Cat's Cradle

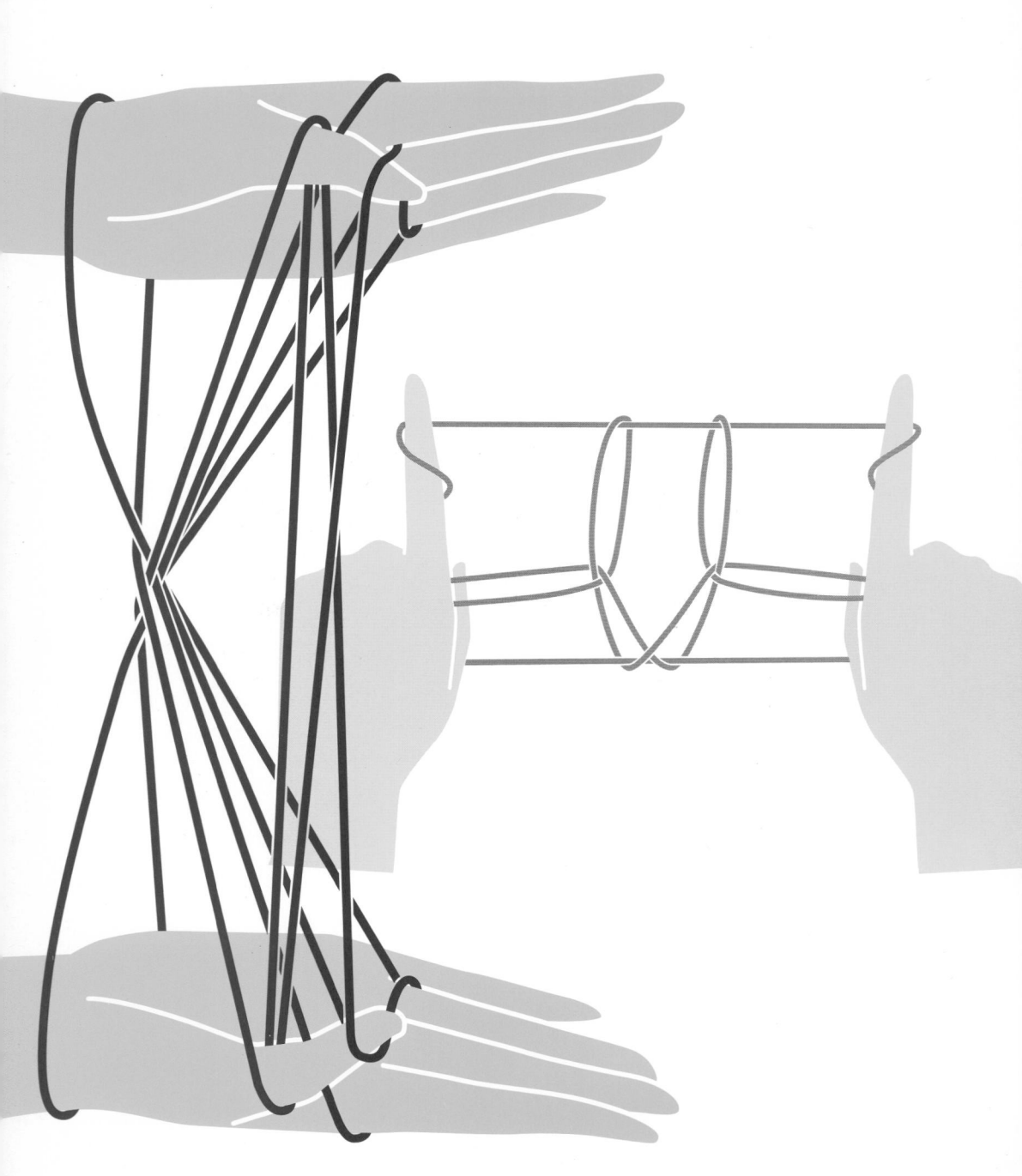

Sophie Collins

Cat's Cradle

Games you can play
with string

Ivy Press

First published in the UK in 2010 by
Ivy Press
210 High Street
Lewes
East Sussex BN7 2NS
United Kingdom
www.ivypress.co.uk

British Library Cataloguing-in-Publication Data
A catalogue record for this book is available
from the British Library

ISBN: 978-1-907332-51-7

This book was conceived, designed and produced by
Ivy Press
Creative Director **Peter Bridgewater**
Publisher **Jason Hook**
Editorial Director **Tom Kitch**
Senior Designer **James Lawrence**
Designer **Sara Nunan**
Illustrators **Janet Baker & Julian Baker (JB Illustrations),
Peters & Zabransky and Ivan Hissey**

Printed in China

Colour origination by Ivy Press Reprographics

10 9 8 7 6 5 4 3 2 1

Contents

6   Introduction

8   Simple Cradles

10   Cat's Cradle
22   Witch's Broom
26   Cup and Saucer/
      Eiffel Tower
31   The Mouse
36   Catch-my-Thumb
40   Man on a Bed
44   Apache Tent
48   Navajo Tent

52   Middling Cradles

54   Navajo Bow
58   Navajo Stars
62   Navajo Lightning
67   The Torres Straits Lizard
70   Jacob's Ladder
76   Two-man Diamonds
81   The Caribou

86   Hard Cradles

88   Leashing the Dogs
94   Caroline Islands Catch
100   The Well
105   The Rabbit
111   The Owl's Net
118   Coral Reef

128   Index

Introduction

From remote Pacific islands to dense African jungle, and from Scottish Highland firesides to Inuit igloos, string games, or 'cat's cradles', played with a metre or so of plain string tied into a closed loop, were an almost universal form of entertainment for hundreds of years. From the middle of the nineteenth century they were arousing academic interest as an aspect of folk art, and ethnographers began to collect rare forms of twists and knots on their travels. As in any other field, the cat's cradle story has its own great names, and among the best known are: Dr Haddon, who assiduously compiled a huge collection of games and made dedicated expeditions to Alaska and South Africa to find more; Dr Furness, who found many entirely new figures in the islands of the Pacific; and his sister, Caroline Furness Jayne, who was inspired to publish the original cat's cradle 'bible', *String Figures and How to Make Them*, in 1906. She wasn't alone; a quick look online will reveal numerous publications dealing with string games, most from the final years of the nineteenth and the first couple of decades of the twentieth centuries. Some are easy to follow; others, sparsely illustrated, less so. Almost all have quaint texts that call for a little interpretation for the modern reader.

Nowadays there is still a dedicated core of string enthusiasts who swap fresh figures, variations and moves with all the enthusiasm of chess players studying a new opening. And, in the playground, cat's cradle has its ups and downs in fashion, enjoying a regular renaissance every few years. This book is for the newcomer to the pleasures of string, offering plenty of simple figures that anyone can make and enjoy, a few how-did-you-do-that tricks that will keep an audience intrigued for

a minute or two and just a handful of sequences that are both long and complex, suitable for whiling away an hour or two, wherever you are.

Cat's cradle has some very special charms: you can practise it anywhere; it can keep bored children entertained for longer than you'd think (and fingers made limber by computer games often mean that kids are adept at completing even complicated figures by themselves); it's truly international – a well-executed cradle will almost always elicit a competitive display of local string virtuosity, even if you find yourself somewhere where you speak not a word of the language; and it's surprisingly soothing, working as effectively as worry beads or meditation when you're feeling tired or tense.

Making Cat's Cradles

The simpler cradles are truly easy to make – the moves come rhythmically and almost automatically after you've made them once or twice. But, as you tackle some of the tougher options, the moves get more complex and you'll find that working out the steps in advance before you actually start shifting the strings proves necessary. For simplicity we've stuck to consistent names throughout – thumb, index finger, middle finger, ring finger and little finger. And, unlike some serious cat's cradle manuals, we've steered clear of shorthand for describing the moves, so even the most advanced cradles are described from the first step to the last without cross-referencing to the other figures. So take up the piece of string provided or use your own one to two-metre (three to six-foot) length, pick a simple figure from the first chapter and get started!

Simple Cradles

There's nothing in this chapter that is too challenging for the novice. It opens with the traditional two-person ever-changing game that, if you've ever played cat's cradle before, is probably the one you remember from childhood. It's long but straightforward (and never-ending, in the sense that it works in a repeating sequence, one player swapping places with the other as you go). Also included are some trick figures – start with the Mouse, which 'runs away' in the final step, and move on to the Man on a Bed. Finally, there's a nod to some Native American figures with an Apache tent and a similar game from the Navajo.

Cat's Cradle

If you remember playing Cat's Cradle at school with your friends, this is probably the version you played. It's a classic, familiar to schoolchildren all over the world. It calls for two people and a bit of practice to get all the steps running smoothly and consists of eight different figures in total, each marking a point in the game; there's something very satisfying about being able to run through the sequence without any mistakes or hesitation. The stages have different names in different cultures, although the actual steps are virtually the same. The Cat's Eye figure, for example, is known as Cow's Eyeball in Korea, and, in Denmark, the Candles step is called the Mirror. Whatever the names, though, it's more or less the same game.

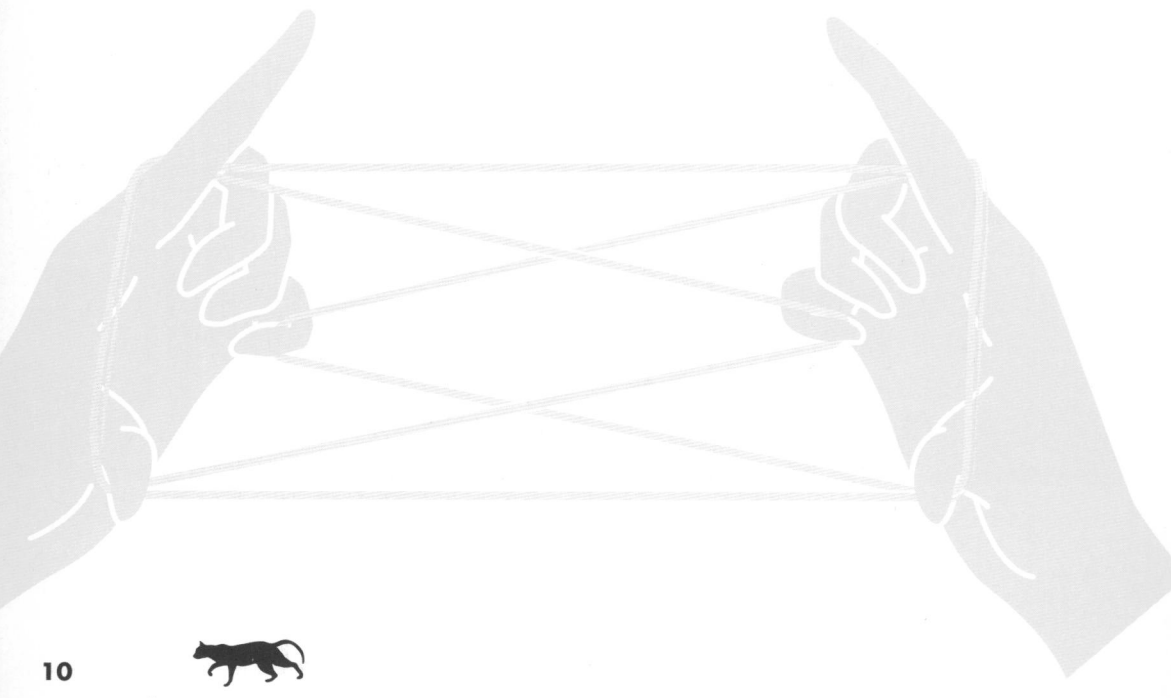

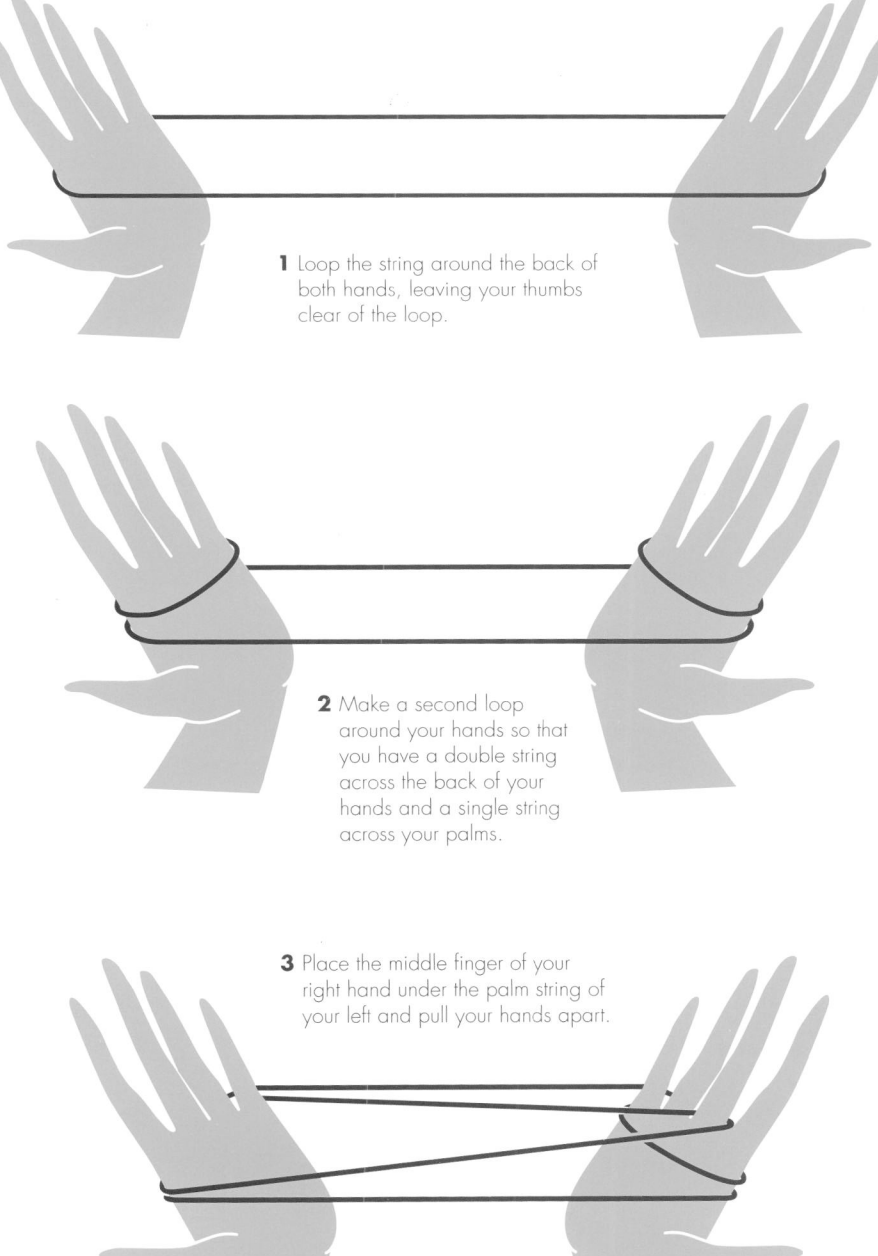

1 Loop the string around the back of both hands, leaving your thumbs clear of the loop.

2 Make a second loop around your hands so that you have a double string across the back of your hands and a single string across your palms.

3 Place the middle finger of your right hand under the palm string of your left and pull your hands apart.

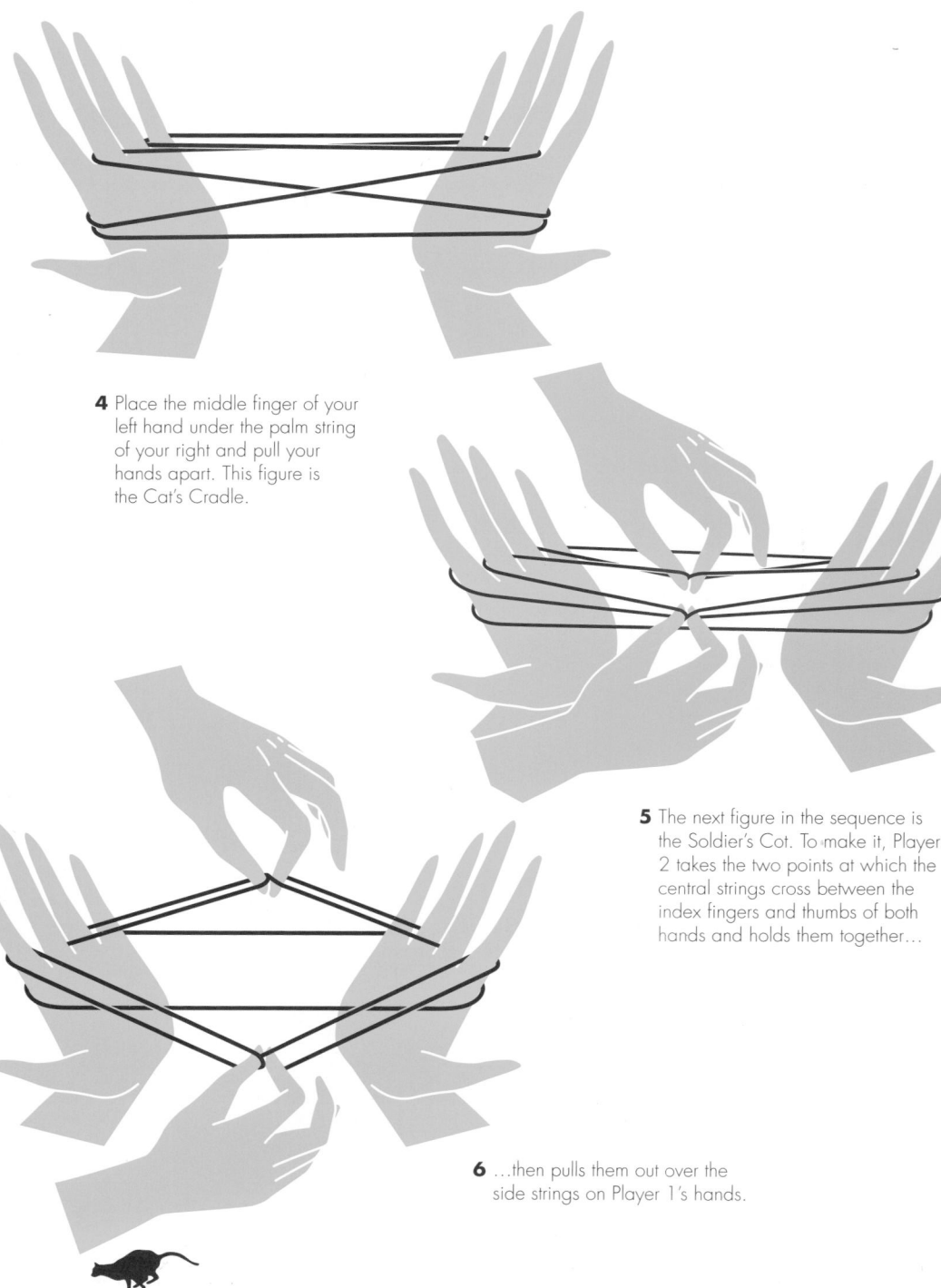

4 Place the middle finger of your
left hand under the palm string
of your right and pull your
hands apart. This figure is
the Cat's Cradle.

5 The next figure in the sequence is
the Soldier's Cot. To make it, Player
2 takes the two points at which the
central strings cross between the
index fingers and thumbs of both
hands and holds them together…

6 …then pulls them out over the
side strings on Player 1's hands.

7 Still holding the central strings, Player 2 pulls them down outside the side strings then pushes them up into the space at the centre of the figure.

8 Player 2 brings their hands upright and pulls them apart and Player 1 drops their hands out of the strings. This completes the Soldier's Cot figure.

9 The next figure is Candles. Player 1 takes the two central crosses formed by the strings at the middle of the figure between the index fingers and thumbs of Player 2's hands.

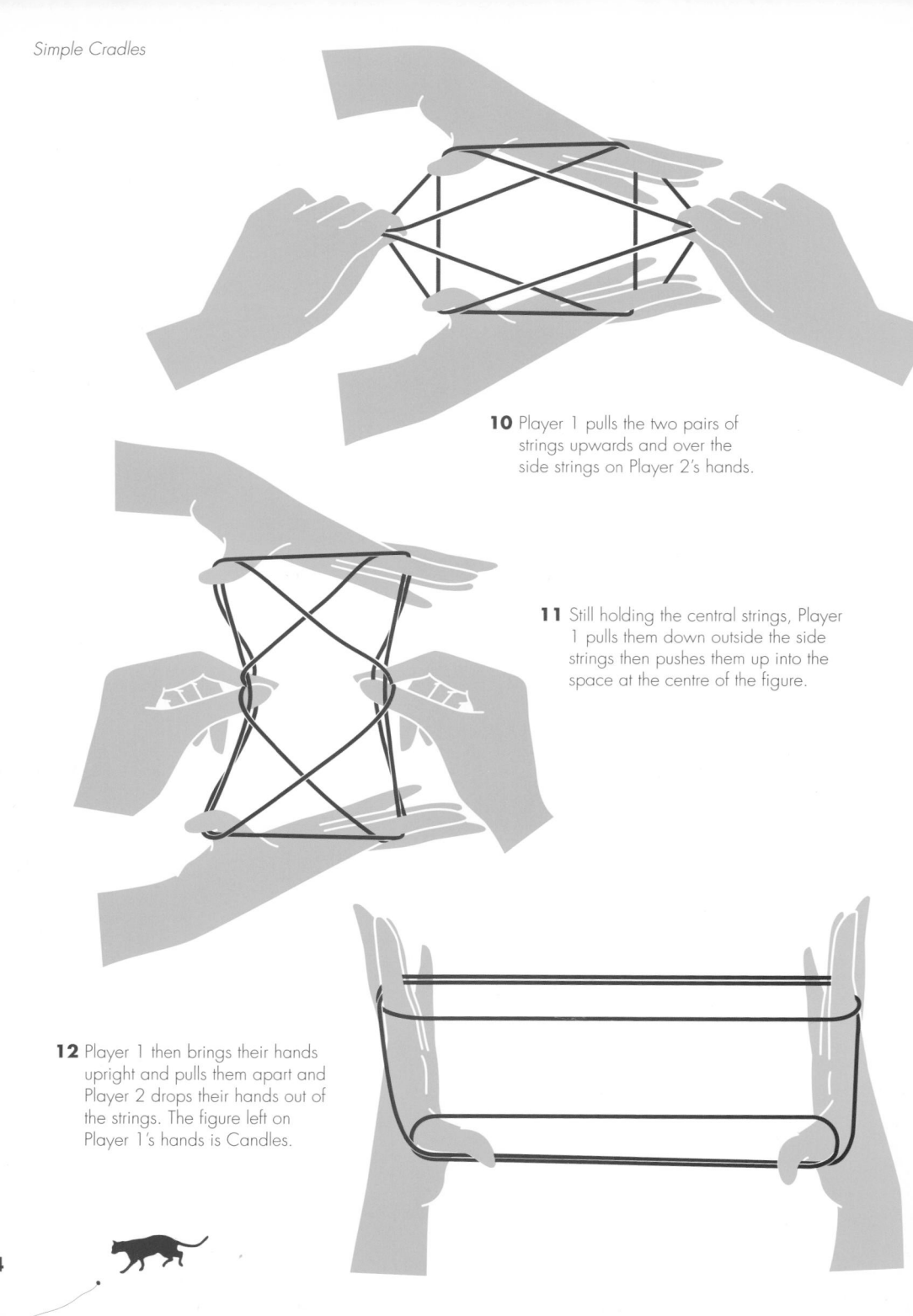

10 Player 1 pulls the two pairs of strings upwards and over the side strings on Player 2's hands.

11 Still holding the central strings, Player 1 pulls them down outside the side strings then pushes them up into the space at the centre of the figure.

12 Player 1 then brings their hands upright and pulls them apart and Player 2 drops their hands out of the strings. The figure left on Player 1's hands is Candles.

13 The next figure In the sequence is the Manger. Player 2 hooks the little finger of their right hand under the string that runs inside Player 1's index fingers and pulls it out and over the thumb strings.

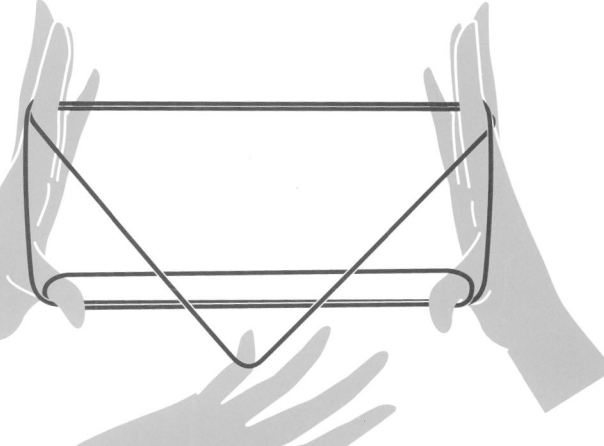

14 Player 2 hooks the little finger of their left hand under the string that runs inside Player 1's thumbs and pulls it out and over the index-finger strings.

15 Now for a slightly tricky move. Still holding the strings firmly in the crook of both little fingers, Player 2 turns their hands over so the palms face downwards, places the thumb and index finger of each hand together and points them through the centres of the two triangles formed in the last step, taking them under the outer strings.

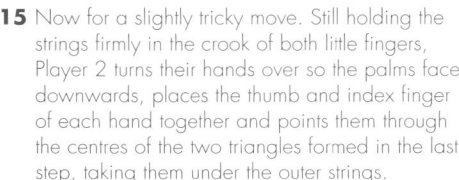

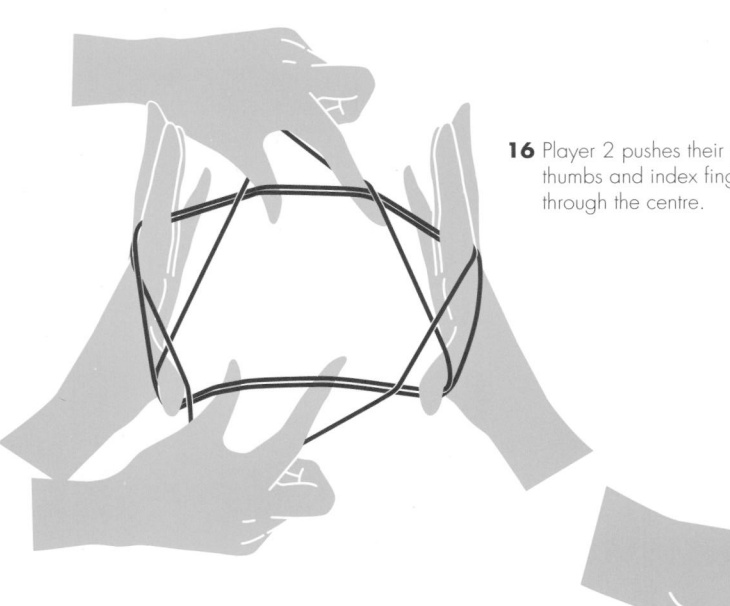

16 Player 2 pushes their joined thumbs and index fingers up through the centre.

17 Player 2 pulls the thumb and index fingers of both hands apart, simultaneously pulling their hands apart while still holding on to the little-finger strings. As they do so, Player 1 drops their hands out of the strings. The figure left on Player 2's hands is the Manger.

18 The next figure in the sequence is Diamonds. Player 1 takes the two crossed pairs of strings leading from the little fingers of Player 2's hands between their thumbs and index fingers...

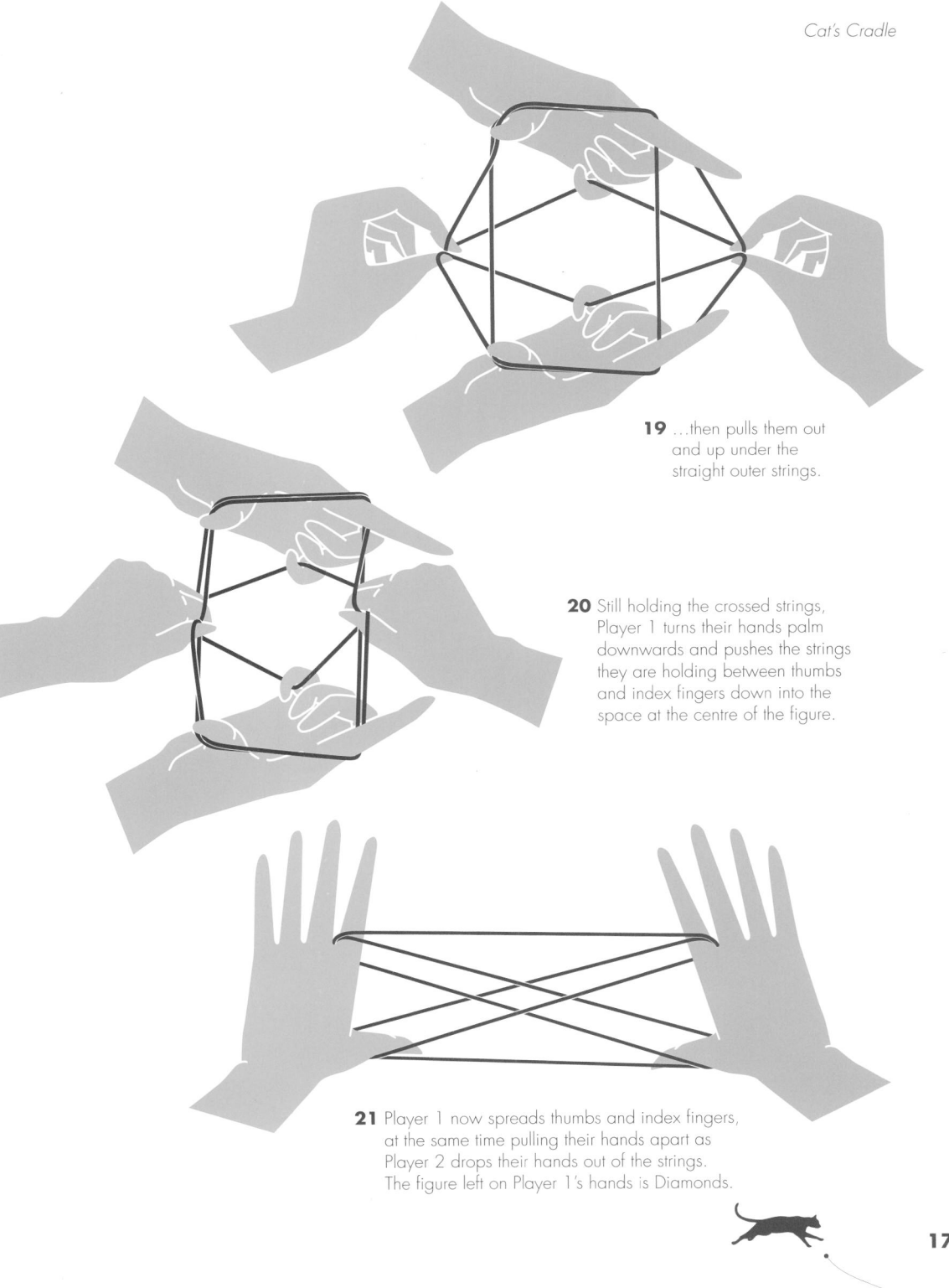

19 …then pulls them out and up under the straight outer strings.

20 Still holding the crossed strings, Player 1 turns their hands palm downwards and pushes the strings they are holding between thumbs and index fingers down into the space at the centre of the figure.

21 Player 1 now spreads thumbs and index fingers, at the same time pulling their hands apart as Player 2 drops their hands out of the strings. The figure left on Player 1's hands is Diamonds.

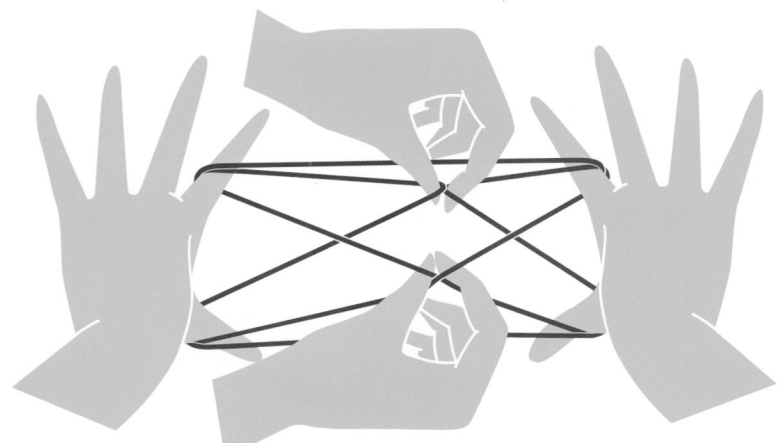

22 The next figure in the sequence is Cat's Eye.
Player 2 takes the two pairs of crossed strings
in the centre of the figure between the joined
thumbs and index fingers of both hands.

23 Player 2 lifts the crossed strings
out over the outer strings...

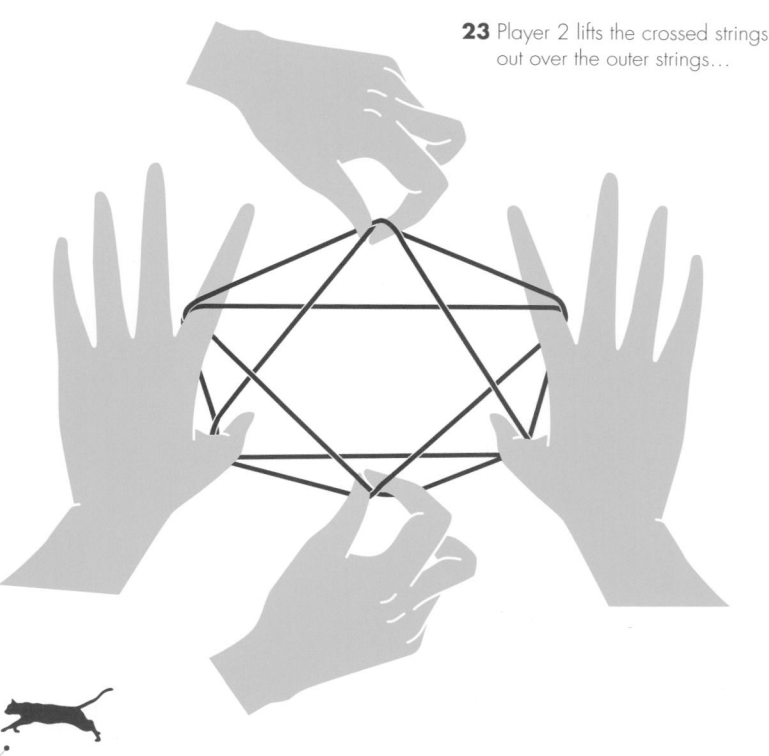

24 …then takes them under and inwards, up into the space at the centre of the figure.

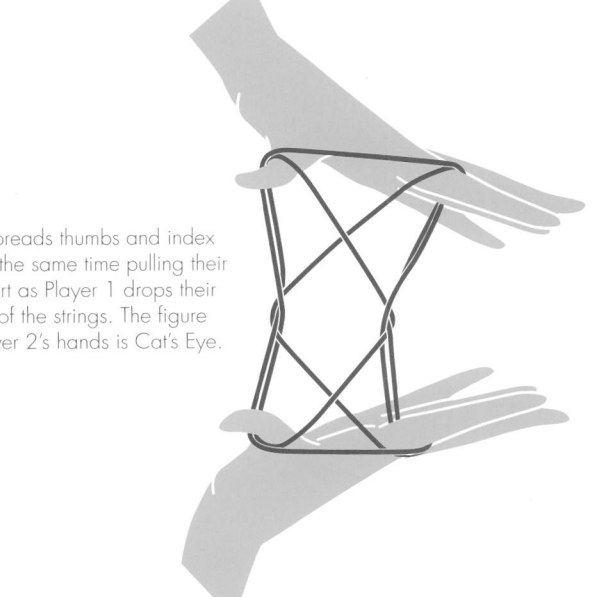

25 Player 2 spreads thumbs and index fingers, at the same time pulling their hands apart as Player 1 drops their hands out of the strings. The figure left on Player 2's hands is Cat's Eye.

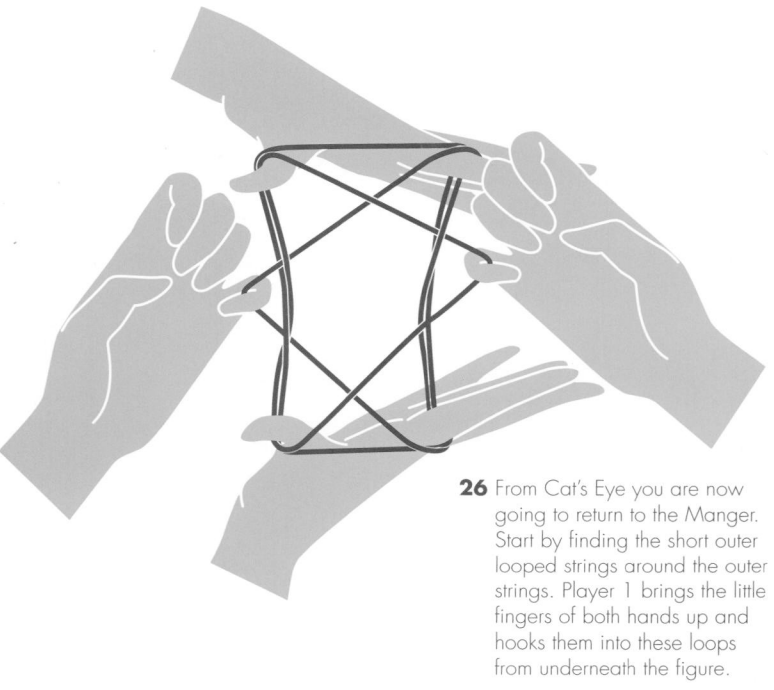

26 From Cat's Eye you are now going to return to the Manger. Start by finding the short outer looped strings around the outer strings. Player 1 brings the little fingers of both hands up and hooks them into these loops from underneath the figure.

27 Player 1 pulls the strings hooked around their little fingers out to the sides of the figure.

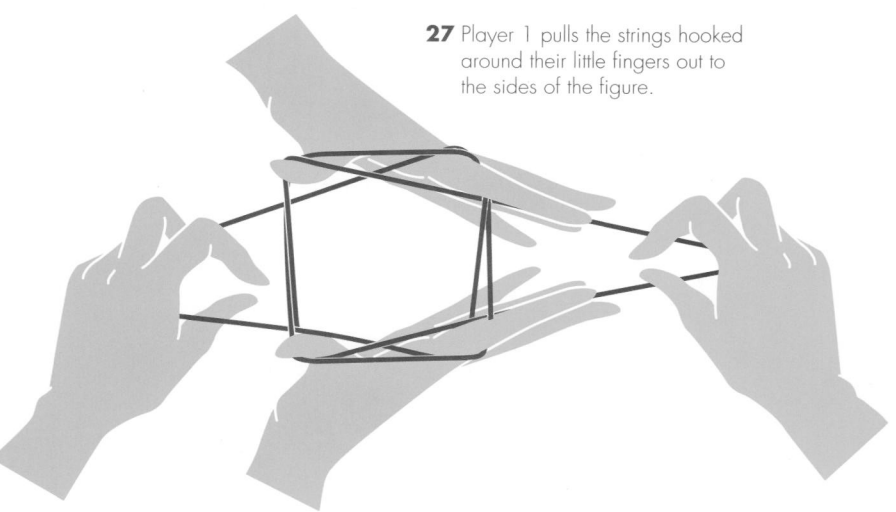

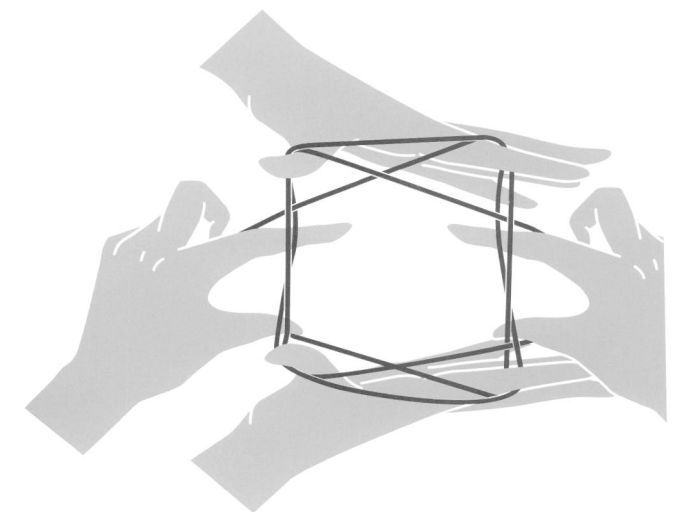

28 Player 1 turns their hands over
and pushes the thumbs and
index fingers of both hands
down into the triangles they've
just formed by pulling out the
little-finger strings, then brings
them under the outer strings
and upwards into the space
at the centre of the figure.

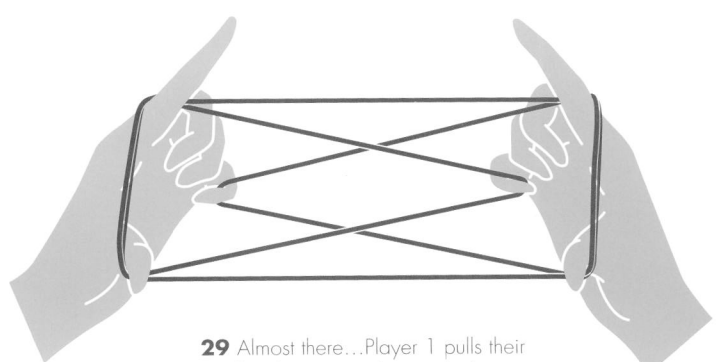

29 Almost there…Player 1 pulls their
hands apart and spreads their
thumbs and index fingers wide.
As they do so, Player 2 drops
their hands out of the strings, and
the figure left on Player 1's hands
is the Manger. The game's come
full circle

If you've practised a lot you'll find that you and your
partner can carry on to repeat the cycle. If you're enjoying
yourselves, you could try a round or two of the complete
sequence against the clock.

Witch's Broom

A neat little string game that earns its name only as you complete the very last step, this is the first of many string figures in which the 'picture' is carried by one hand with just a loop or two supporting it on the other – a basic structure that has numerous variations. In Jayne's 1906 collection there is a wide selection of string games named after tents and fishing nets with similar forms to this, but the actual name of this game is probably European, because it's mainly in European folklore that witches fly about on broomsticks.

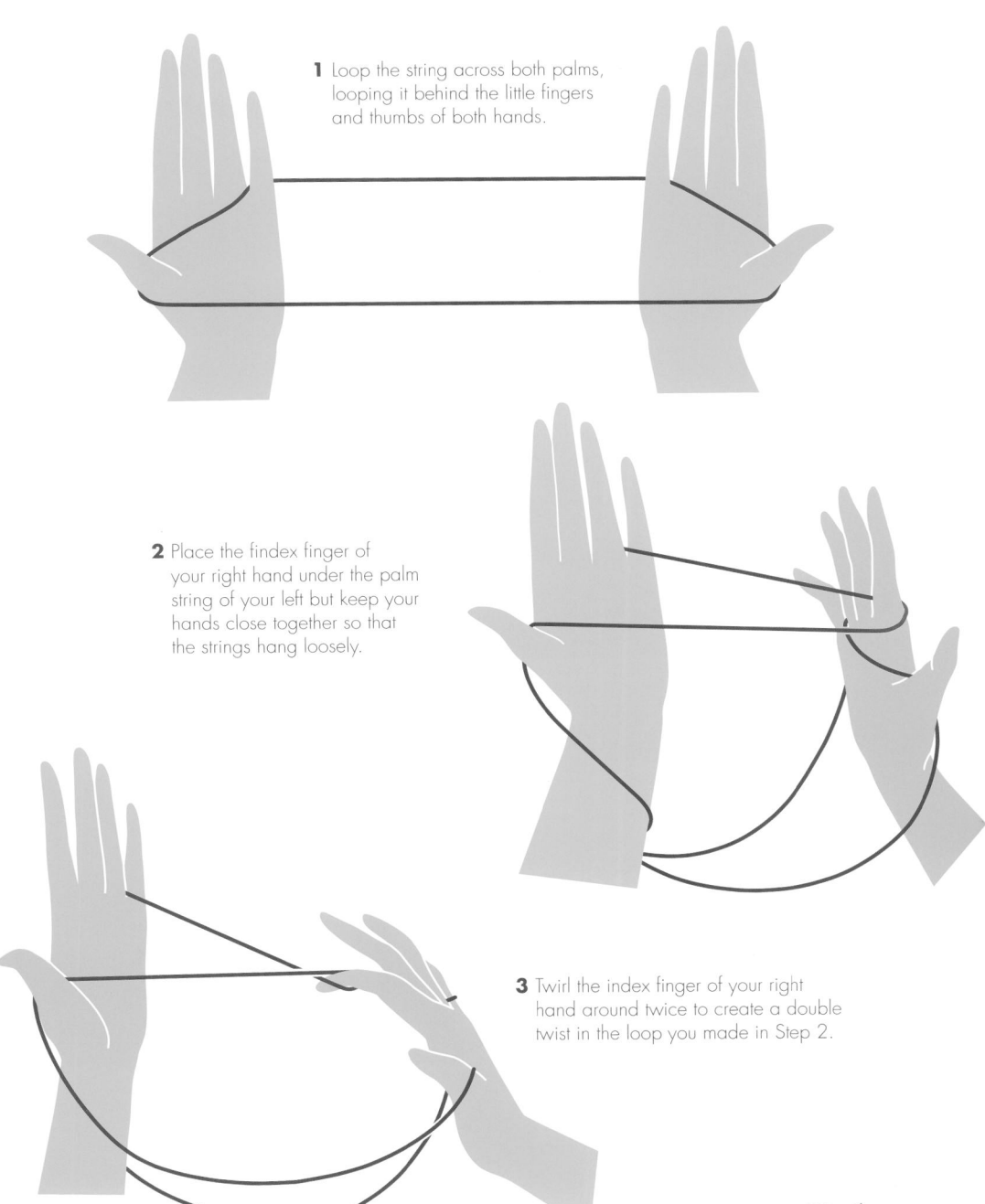

1 Loop the string across both palms, looping it behind the little fingers and thumbs of both hands.

2 Place the findex finger of your right hand under the palm string of your left but keep your hands close together so that the strings hang loosely.

3 Twirl the index finger of your right hand around twice to create a double twist in the loop you made in Step 2.

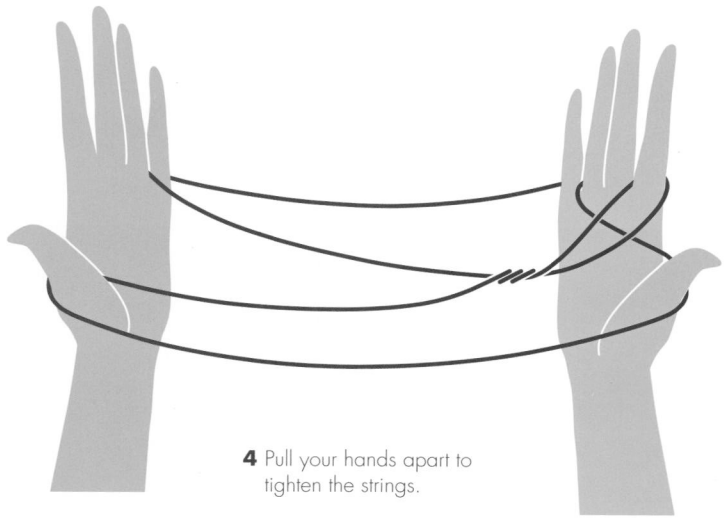

4 Pull your hands apart to
tighten the strings.

5 Reaching through the twisted
loop that you've made, place
the index finger of your left
hand under the palm string
of your right.

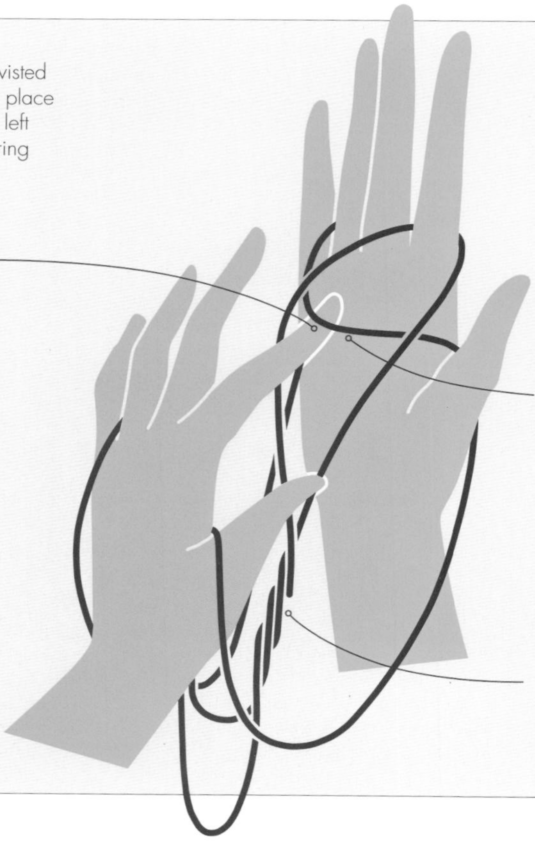

Push the index finger...

...under the
palm string

Make sure the
double twist
doesn't come loose

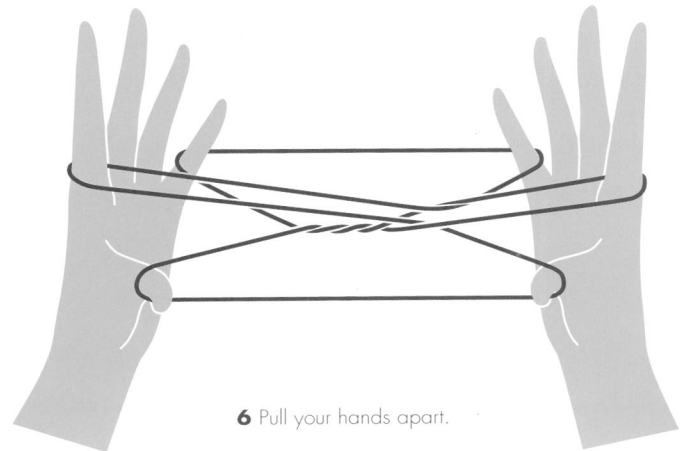

6 Pull your hands apart.

7 Carefully drop the loops from the thumb and little finger of your right hand and pull your hands apart again to create the Witch's Broom.

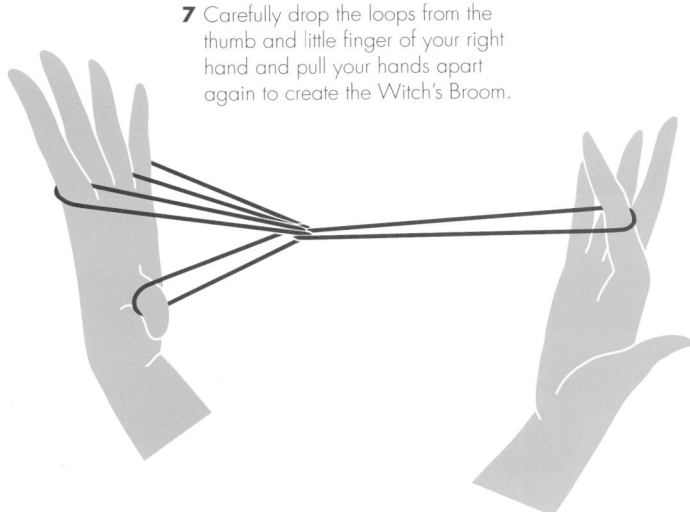

Cup and Saucer/Eiffel Tower

This simple sequence sees you first creating a cup-and-saucer outline then, with a couple of neat moves, transforming them into a convincing rendition of the Eiffel Tower. You'll need to call in an extra hand from a friend for the final steps (unless you're happy to take the topmost string in your teeth), but the steps are easy to learn, and it's an impressive first two-figure game to show off to your friends.

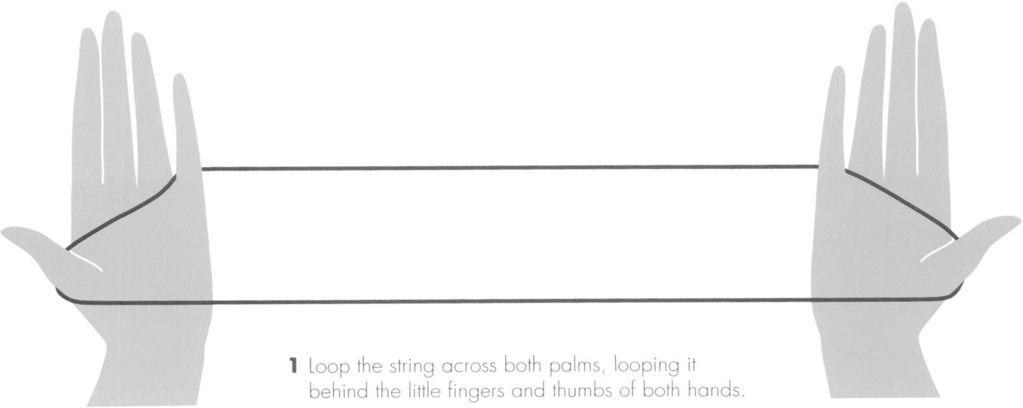

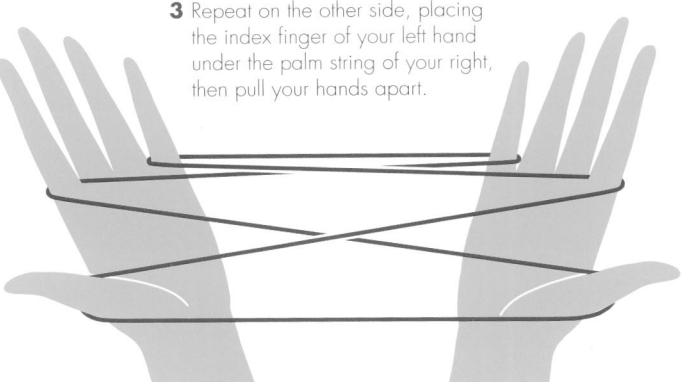

1 Loop the string across both palms, looping it behind the little fingers and thumbs of both hands.

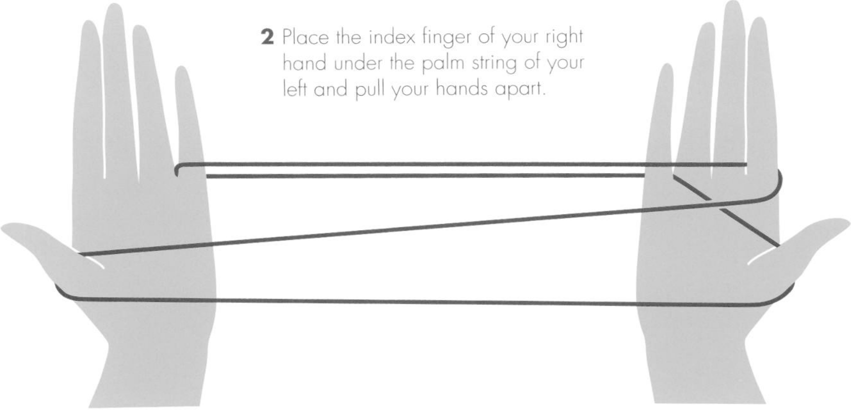

2 Place the index finger of your right hand under the palm string of your left and pull your hands apart.

3 Repeat on the other side, placing the index finger of your left hand under the palm string of your right, then pull your hands apart.

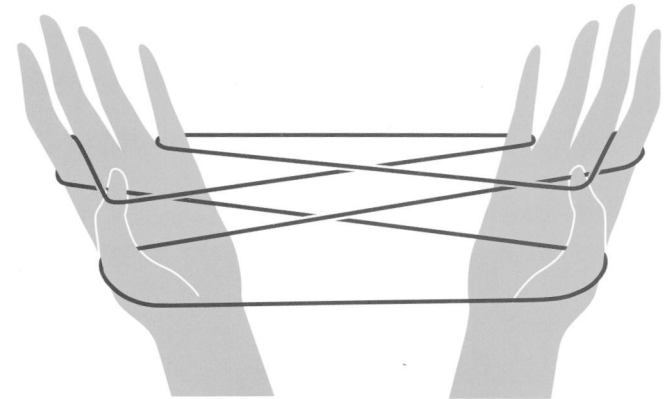

4 Reach both your thumbs over the top of
the cradle and hook them under the string
on the far side of your index fingers.

5 Move your thumbs back to the
'open palm' position. You will
have two loops of string on each.

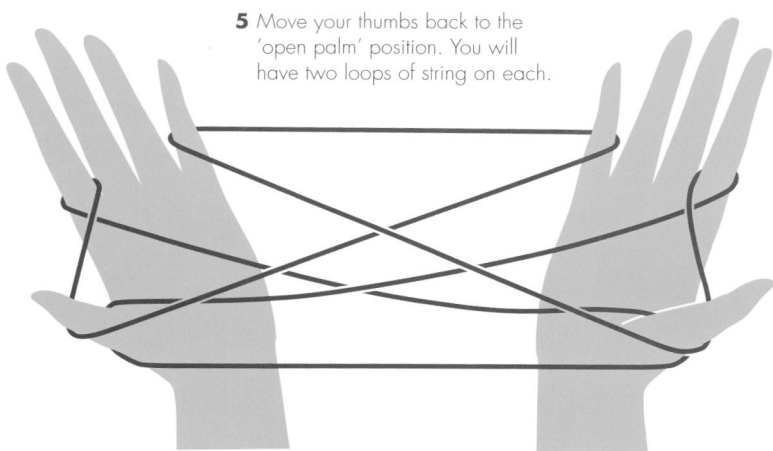

6 Slip the lower loops off your
thumbs by passing them over
the top ones without releasing
the latter. If you're dexterous you
may be able to do this yourself;
if you find it too tricky, ask a
friend to help you.

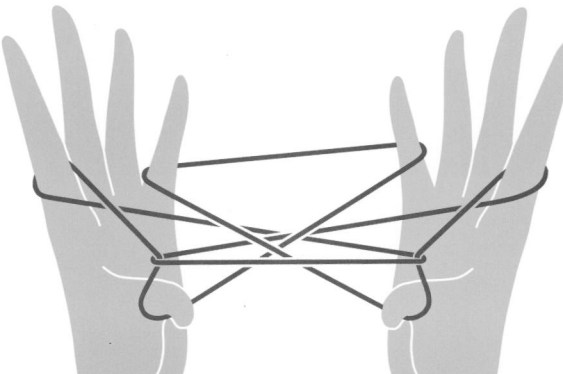

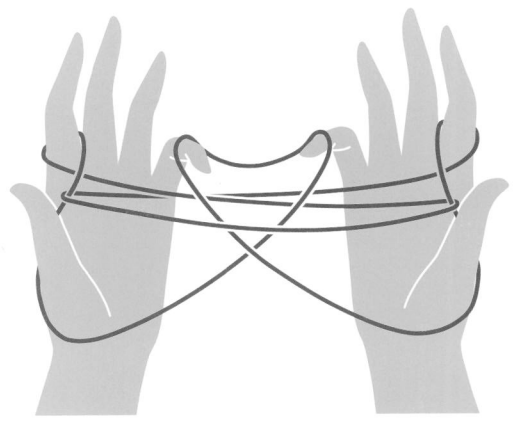

7 Carefully drop the loops off your little fingers.

8 Pull your hands apart.

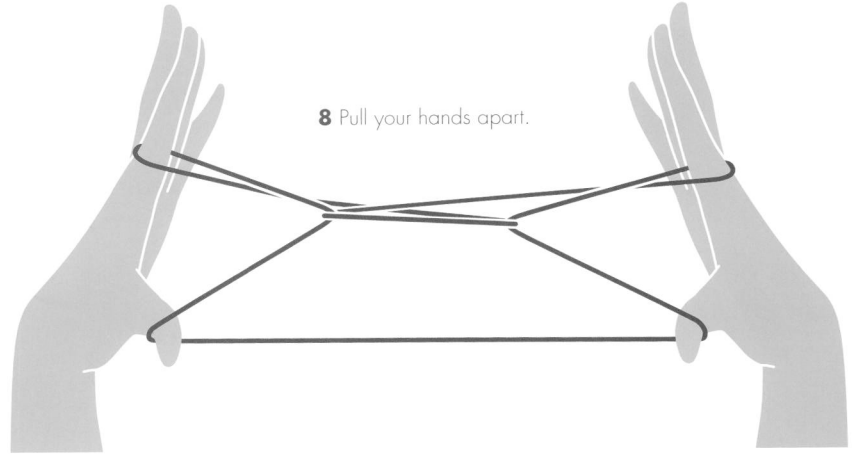

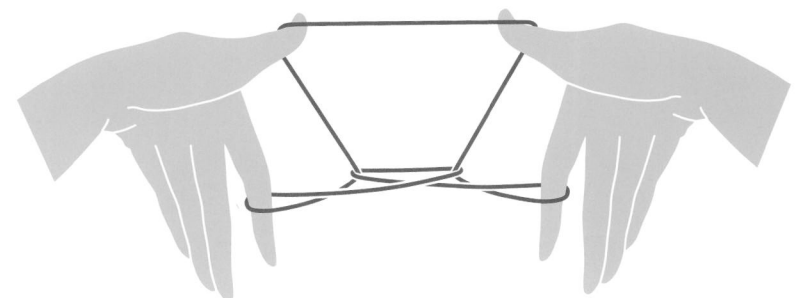

9 The cup and saucer is now complete – if you turn your hands so that your thumbs are pointing upwards, the shape will show clearly.

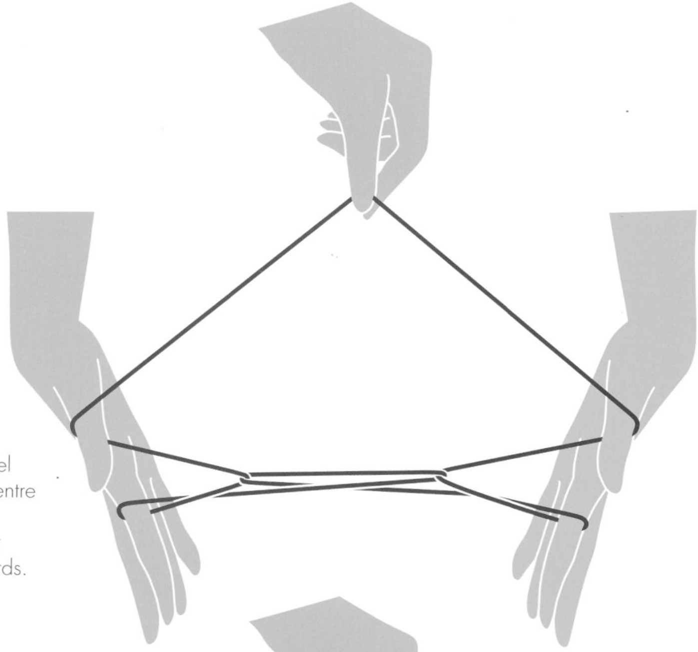

10 Now turn the pattern into the Eiffel Tower: ask a friend to take the centre of the string that makes up the topline of the cup between finger and thumb and pull gently upwards.

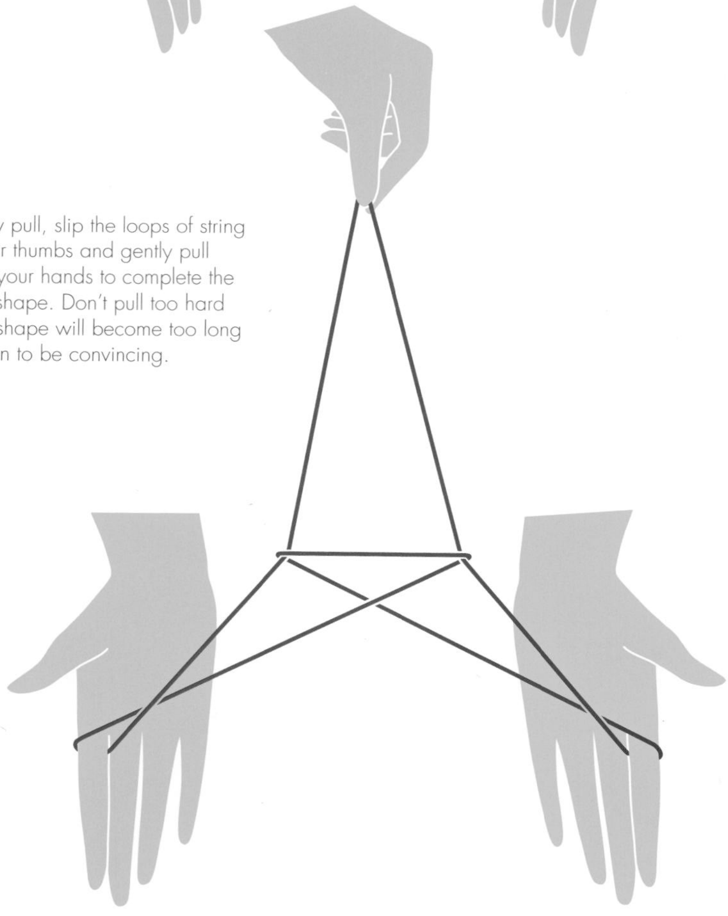

11 As they pull, slip the loops of string off your thumbs and gently pull down your hands to complete the tower shape. Don't pull too hard or the shape will become too long and thin to be convincing.

The Mouse

This is one of several variations in which the string is carefully looped and pulled around the left hand and then whisked away in a single movement at the end. You can show it off by building the 'mouse' gradually, giving a commentary as you make the loops over each finger – 'And here's his back leg…' and so on – and then finish by saying, 'He's seen a cat! And…' (dropping the final loop from your thumb and pulling the string to unravel your mouse) '…now he's run away!' Small children, and plenty of adults, love this denouement, so practise until you can do all the steps smoothly before you show it off. If you knit, you'll find that the loops around the fingers are created in a similar way to casting on wool.

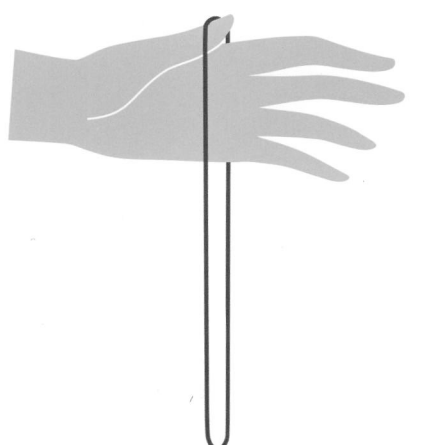

1 Hold your left hand horizontally in front of you, palm down, and drape the loop of string across the back of it with the loop hanging down over the outer edges of your thumb and little finger.

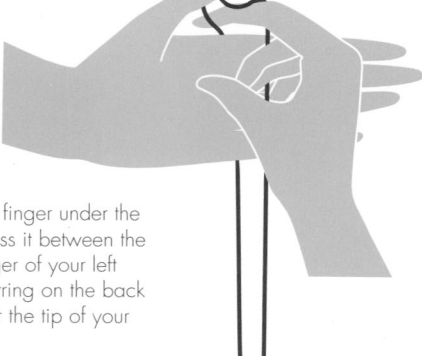

2 Push your right index finger under the loop from the left, pass it between the thumb and index finger of your left hand and hook the string on the back of the left hand under the tip of your index finger.

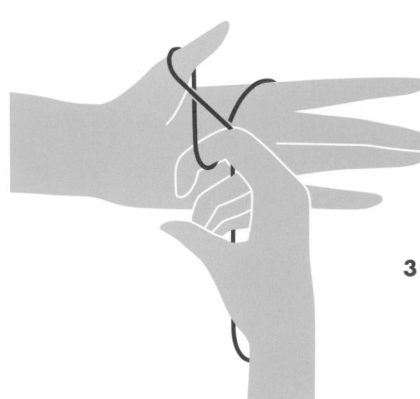

3 Pull the portion of string hooked in your right index through the gap between the left thumb and index finger and bring it under the front loop, still hooked around the right index finger.

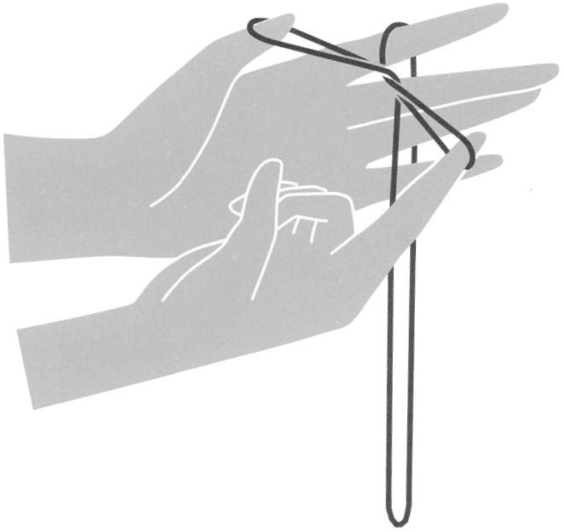

4 Pull the loop around your right
index finger out slightly and give
it a single anticlockwise twist.

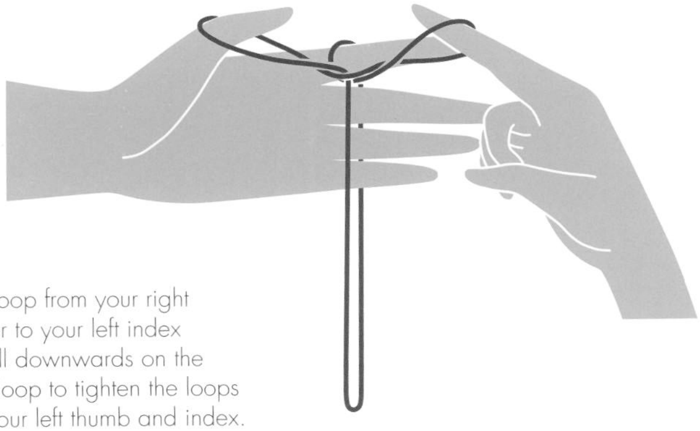

5 Shift the loop from your right
hand over to your left index
finger. Pull downwards on the
hanging loop to tighten the loops
around your left thumb and index.

6 Repeat the process, this time passing
your right index finger between the
index and middle fingers of your
left hand.

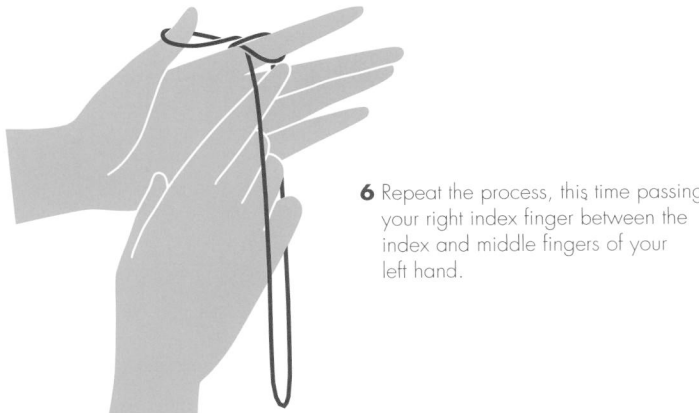

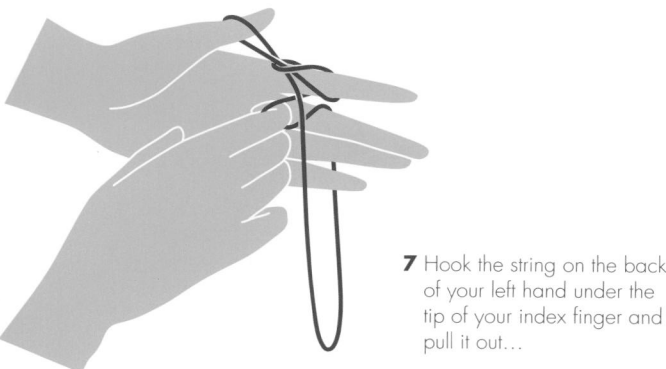

7 Hook the string on the back of your left hand under the tip of your index finger and pull it out…

8 …then give it a twist before transferring it from your right index finger on to your left middle finger.

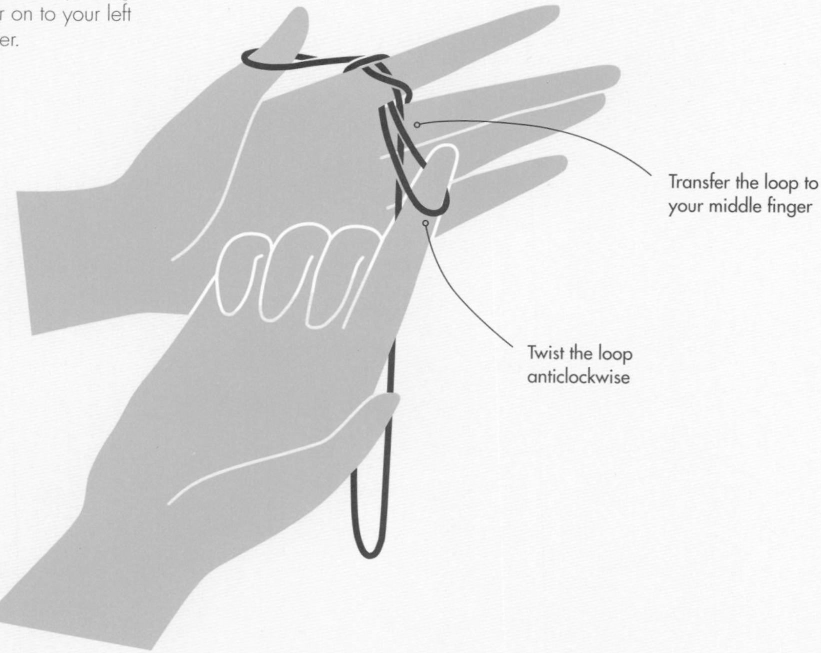

Transfer the loop to your middle finger

Twist the loop anticlockwise

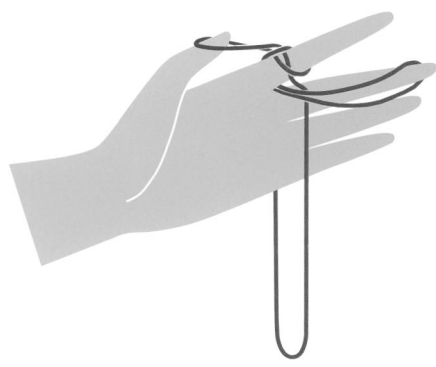

9 When all three loops are in place around the thumb, index and middle fingers of your left hand, pull down on the loop to tighten them.

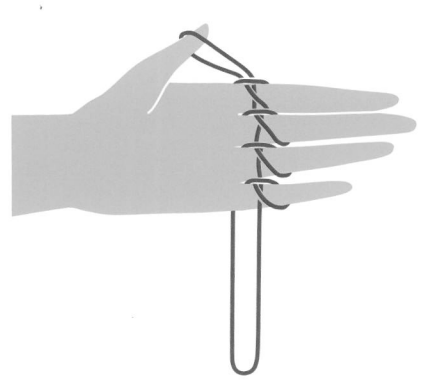

10 Repeat the process, this time pulling the loop between the middle and ring fingers of your left hand, and transferring the twisted loop from your right index finger on to your left ring finger. Then repeat the process, this time pulling the loop between the ring and little fingers of your left hand, and transferring the twisted loop from your right index on to your left little finger. You now have loops around the thumb and all four fingers of your left hand.

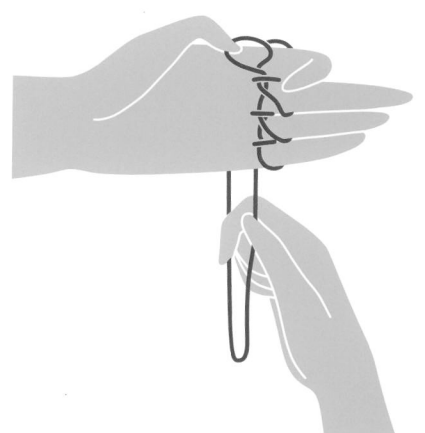

11 To unravel the figure, slip your left thumb out of its loop, and use the thumb and index finger of your right hand to pull downwards on the hanging string nearest you. As you do so, the whole figure will unravel and the mouse will 'run away'.

35

Catch-my-thumb

Credited to the Osage tribe of Native Americans by both Jayne and Haddon in their books, this simple thumb catch was also recorded by folk-craft enthusiasts in nineteenth-century eastern Europe and an equally straightforward variant was noted in the islands of the Pacific. You can learn it in a moment or two, and it's a good choice if you're limbering up to make some of the more complex string figures.

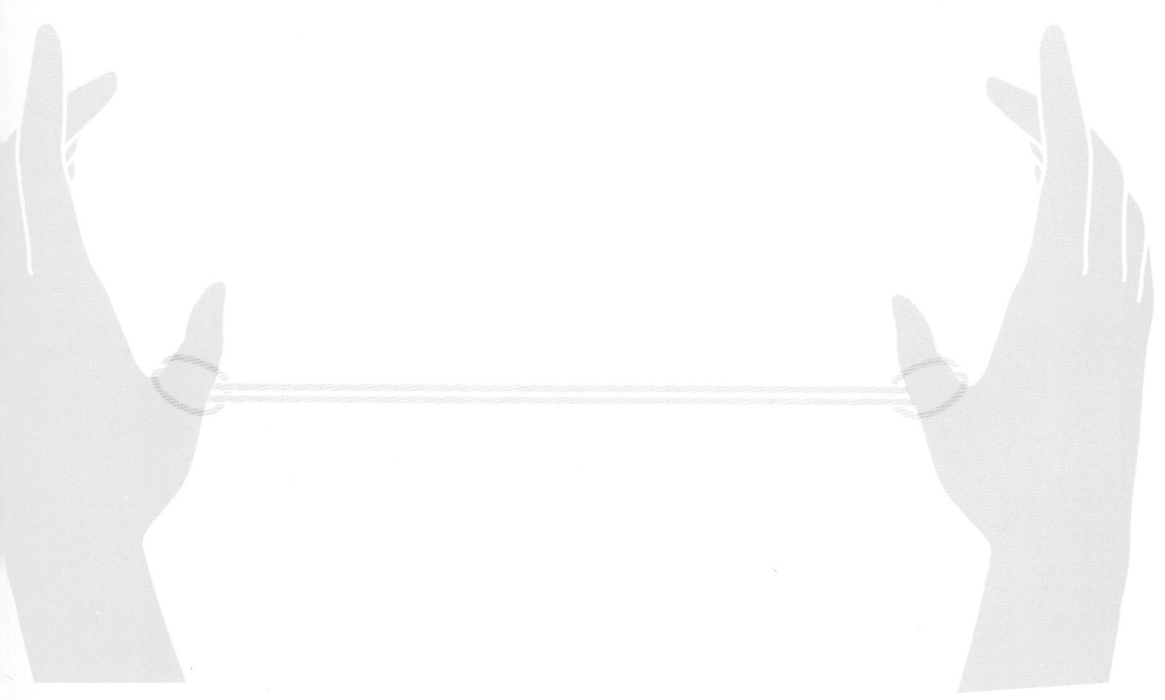

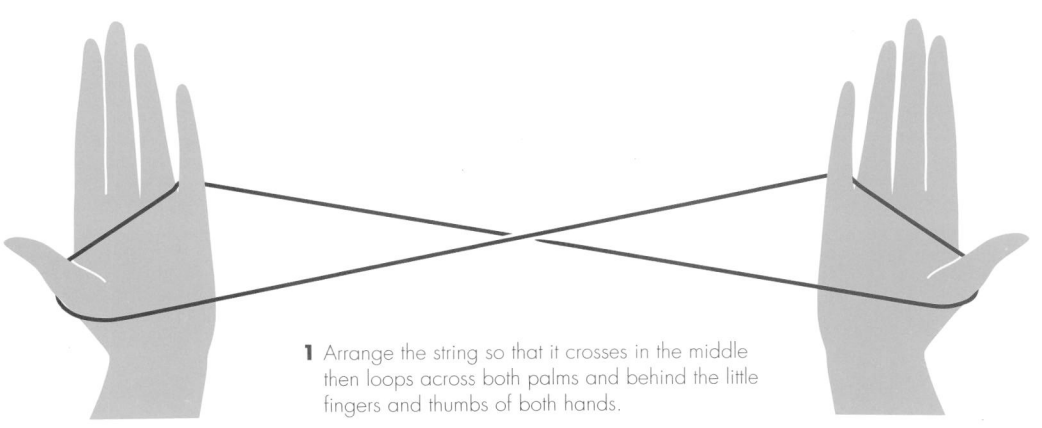

1 Arrange the string so that it crosses in the middle then loops across both palms and behind the little fingers and thumbs of both hands.

2 Place the index finger of your right hand under the palm string of your left and pull your hands apart.

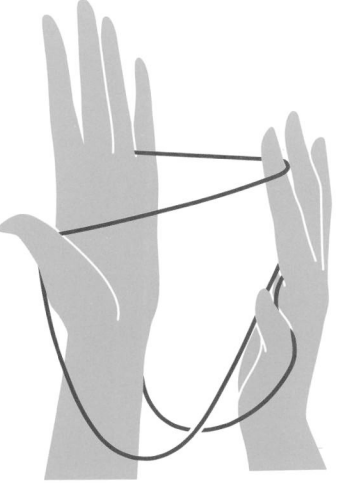

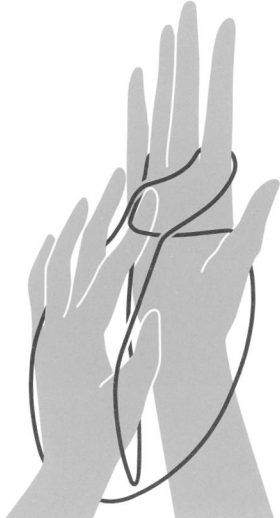

3 Repeat on the other side, placing the index finger of your left hand under the palm string of your right.

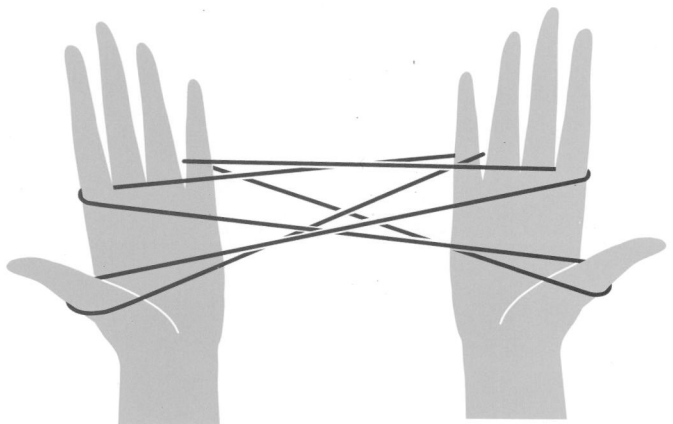

4 Pull your hands apart – you'll have loops of string around your little fingers, index fingers and thumbs.

5 Turn your thumbs away from you, pushing them down into the loops around your index fingers, and bend them so that you're holding the furthest thumb strings and the nearest index-finger strings in the crooks of your thumbs.

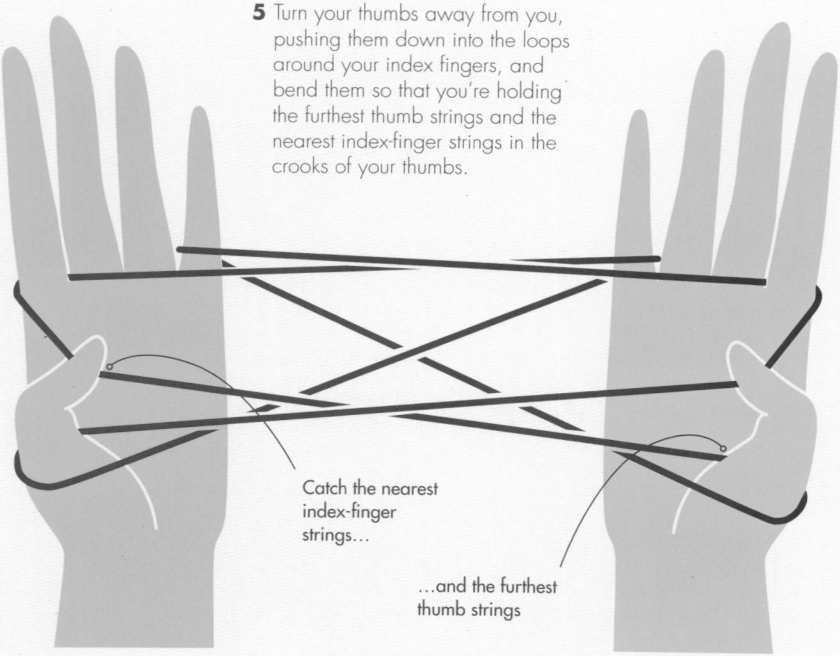

Catch the nearest index-finger strings...

...and the furthest thumb strings

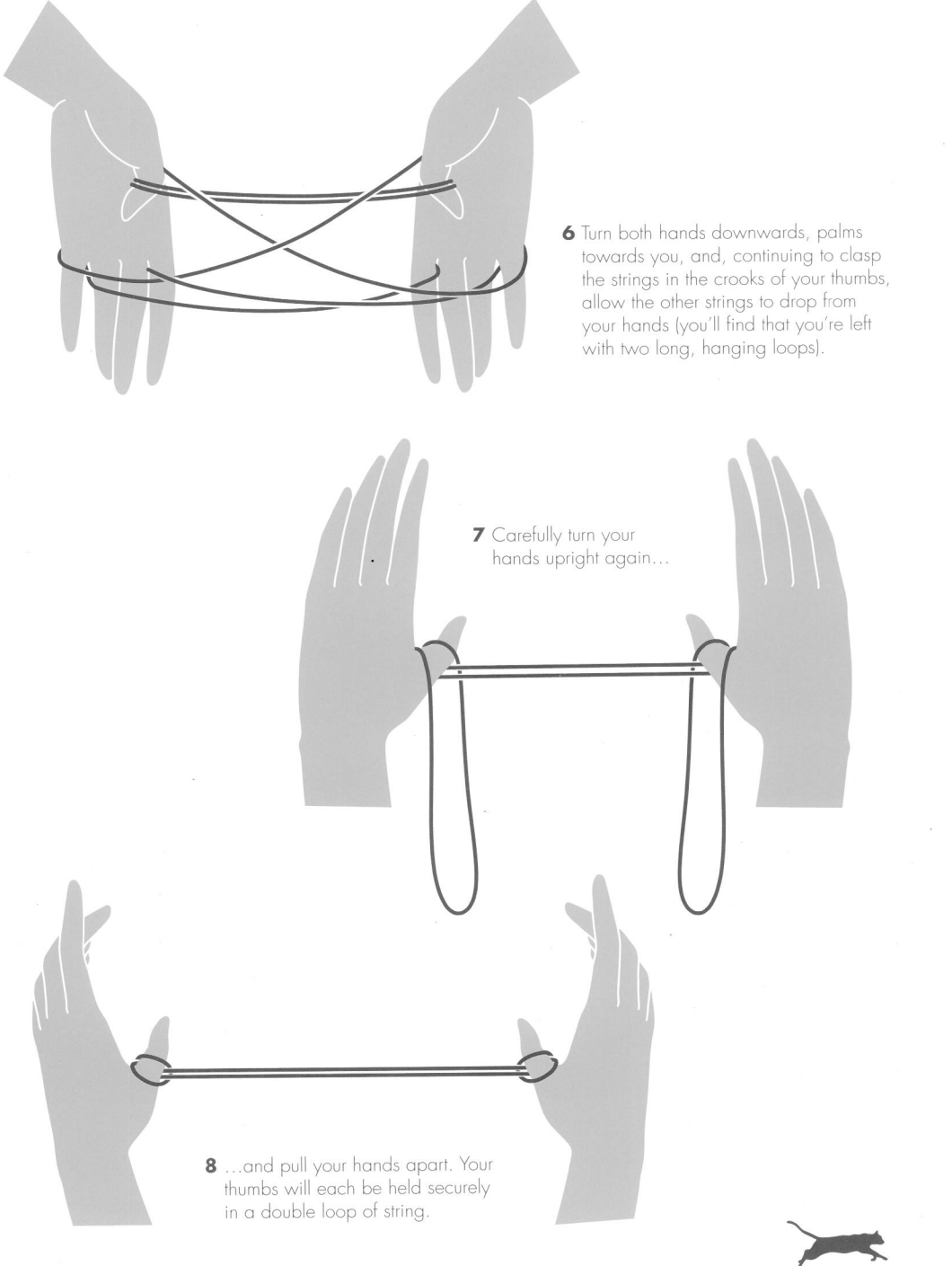

6 Turn both hands downwards, palms towards you, and, continuing to clasp the strings in the crooks of your thumbs, allow the other strings to drop from your hands (you'll find that you're left with two long, hanging loops).

7 Carefully turn your hands upright again…

8 …and pull your hands apart. Your thumbs will each be held securely in a double loop of string.

Man on a Bed

Like the Mouse on pages 31–5, Man on a Bed is a string game
in which you build up a picture then unravel it in the final step
with a single tug on the string. Originating in the islands of the
Torres Straits, Man on a Bed was originally accompanied by
a simple chant in which the man lies down on the bed and falls
asleep. In the final step, predictably enough, the loops are slipped
off the little fingers, the 'bed' breaks, and the man falls down.

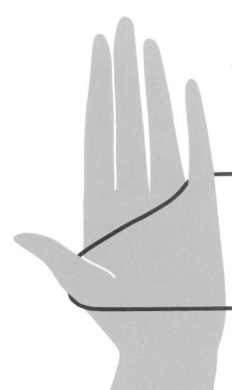
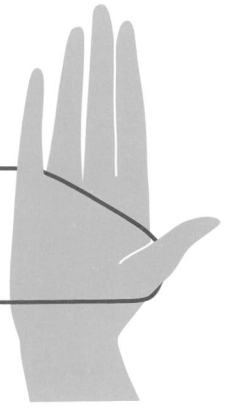

1 Loop the string across both palms and behind the little fingers and thumbs of both hands.

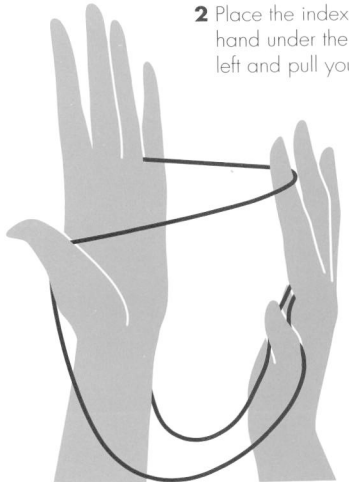

2 Place the index finger of your right hand under the palm string of your left and pull your hands apart.

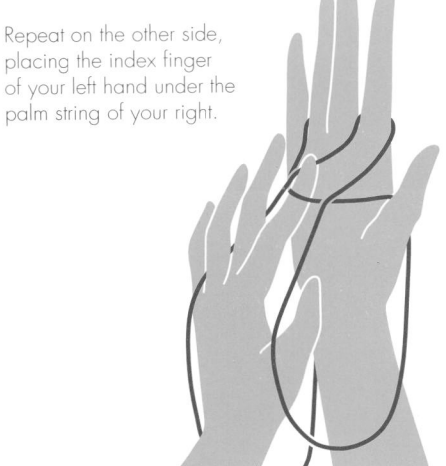

3 Repeat on the other side, placing the index finger of your left hand under the palm string of your right.

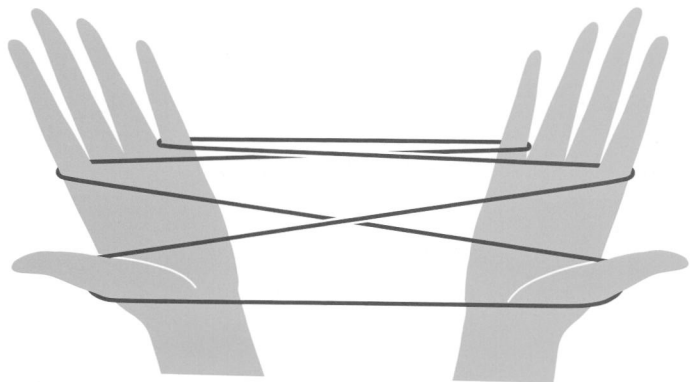

4 Pull your hands apart – you'll have loops around your little fingers, index fingers and thumbs.

5 Move your thumbs away from you, taking them under the loops around the index fingers, catch the little-finger string nearest you on the backs of your thumbs (shown here on the left hand), and return your thumbs to their original positions (shown here on the right hand).

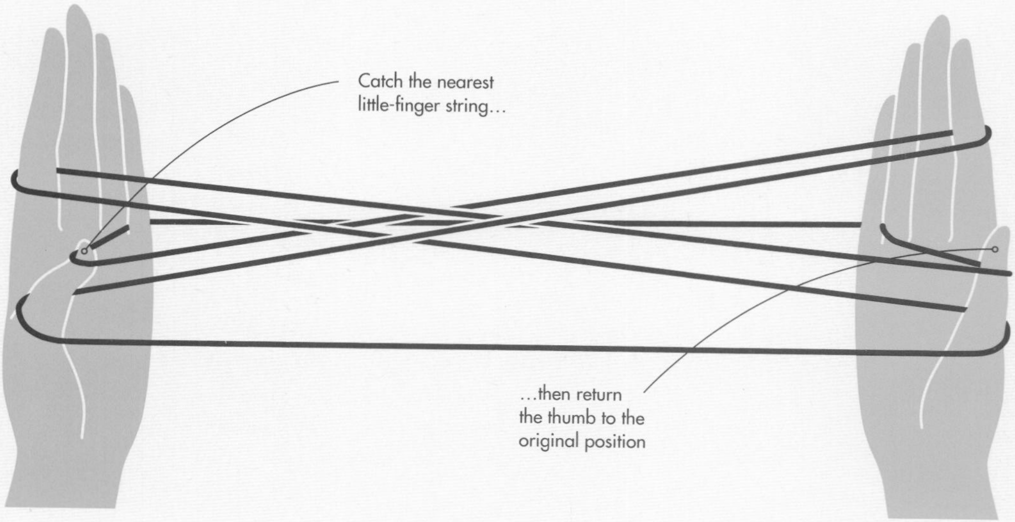

Catch the nearest little-finger string...

...then return the thumb to the original position

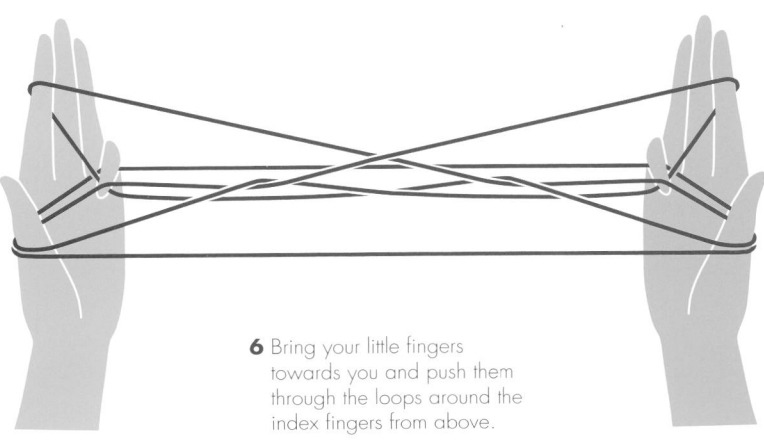

6 Bring your little fingers towards you and push them through the loops around the index fingers from above.

7 Use your little fingers to pick up the string around your thumbs furthest from you and return them to their original position. Release the loops from the index fingers. Looking at the figure from above, the man is now on his bed. To unravel the pattern, simply slip the loops from your little fingers and the strings will fall away.

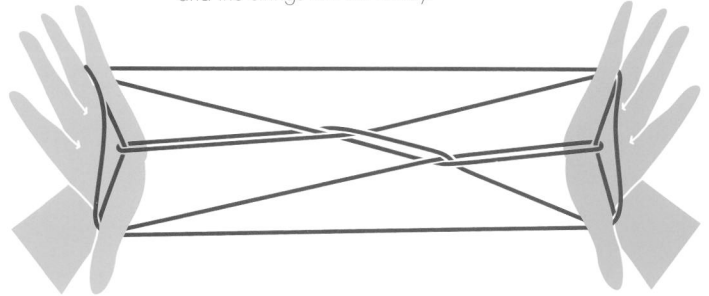

Apache Tent

In this figure, most of the steps are worked on one hand by the other, creating a broad-based but triangular end result as the right hand drops horizontally, palm up, to make the tent. The tent pattern is less apparent in the end result of this figure than it is in the Navajo-derived tent on pages 48–51 – but, on the plus side, the figure is easier to do.

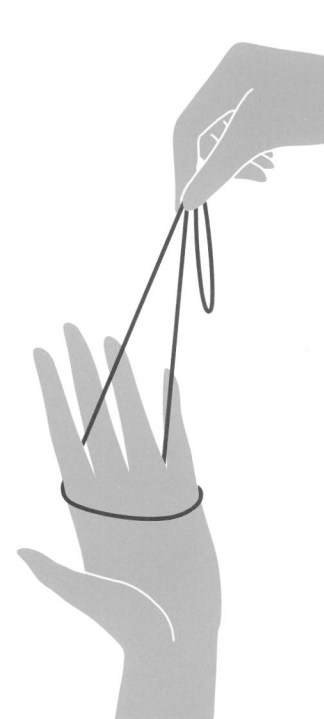

1 Drape the string around the palm of your left hand then hold the hand upwards. With your right hand gather the loose string up behind the left hand and pull the string sides through the gaps between your left thumb and index finger and between your left ring finger and little finger.

2 Let the loop hang down in front of the palm string on your left hand.

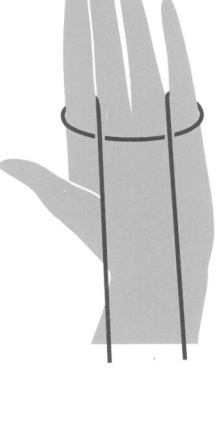

3 Use the index finger of your right hand to reach under the palm string on your left hand and hook the two strings of the loop with it, bringing them down behind the palm string.

4 Pull the loop right through and release it so that it is hanging down behind the palm string on your left hand.

5 Push your right hand through the hanging loop from underneath and bring it up so that it is palm-to-palm with your left hand. Slip the little finger of your right hand through the string at the point at which it comes between the little and ring fingers of your left hand.

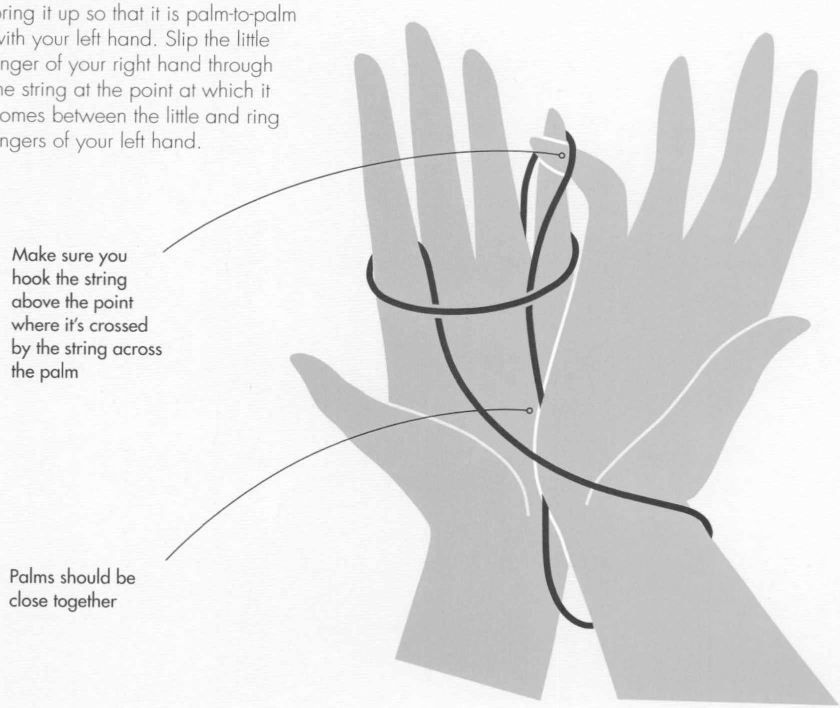

Make sure you hook the string above the point where it's crossed by the string across the palm

Palms should be close together

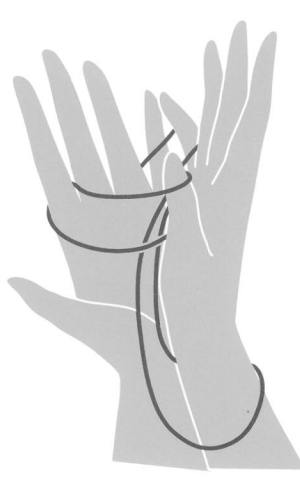

6 Now slip the thumb of your right hand through the string at the point at which it comes between the index and middle fingers of your left hand. You now have loops over the little finger and the thumb of your right hand.

7 To create the tent, separate your hands, keeping the string in position around the back of the right wrist – don't let it move upwards – then move your hands, while holding them apart, so that the strings are taut and your left hand is palm down and your right hand, pointing away from you, palm up. The shape of the tent will become clear.

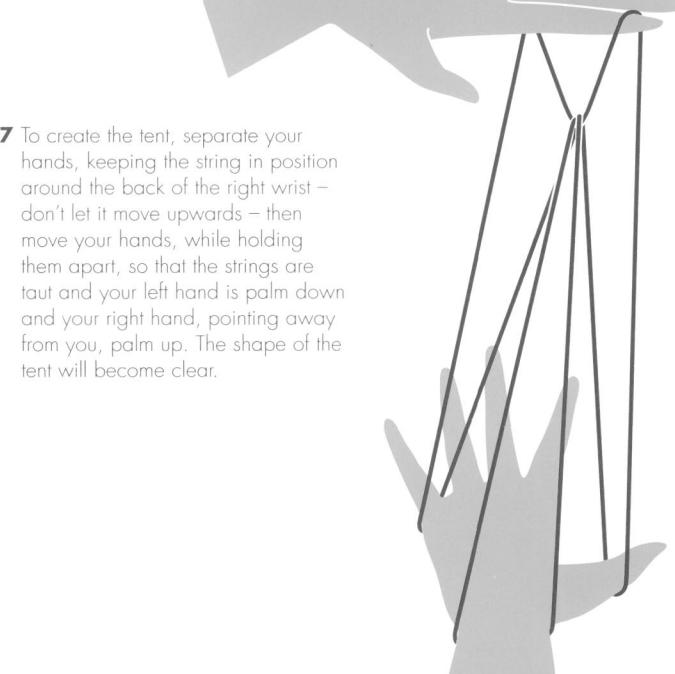

Navajo Tent

Like the Apache Tent on pages 44–47, this figure is formed
by a series of moves on one hand and then completed by a final
move takes your hands from vertical to horizontal. Broad-based
and narrowing to a point with a loop of string representing the
poles, the final shape is a convincing tent. Be careful not to let any
of the finger loops slip as you move your left hand palm up at the
last stage – the whole figure will immediately fall to pieces if you
do, and you'll have to go back to the beginning.

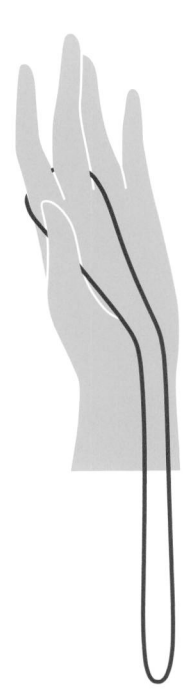

1 Drape the string around the index and middle fingers of your left hand so that the loop falls down across your palm.

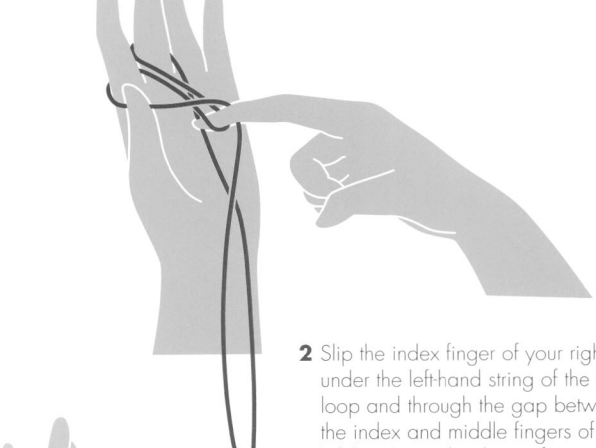

2 Slip the index finger of your right hand under the left-hand string of the main loop and through the gap between the index and middle fingers of your left hand. Hook a loop of string through from the back of the hand to the front.

3 Continue to pull until the full length of the string has come through the fingers — you'll be left with a tight loop around the index and middle fingers of your left hand and the main length of the string hanging down from behind it in front of your left palm.

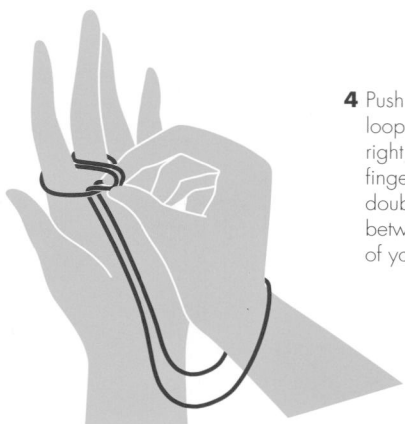

4 Push your right hand through the hanging loop so that you're holding it around your right wrist, and use the thumb and index finger of your right hand to pick up the double string where it emerges from between the index and middle fingers of your left hand.

5 Pull the strings out with your right hand as far as you can. As you reach the bottom of the loop, slip your right wrist and hand out of the loop to complete the move.

6 You now have loops around the index and middle fingers of your left hand, passing into a twist of string beneath which two loops hang down across your left-hand palm.

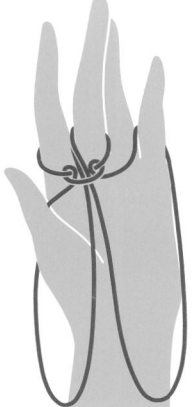

7 With your right hand pick up the nearest of the two hanging loops and put it over the thumb of your left hand. Then pick up the other loop and put it over the little finger of your left hand.

8 With the thumb and index finger of your right hand pull the string that goes straight across the front of the four hanging strings on your left hand and pull it outwards until the strings are taut.

9 Move your left hand into a horizontal position, palm up and fingers facing away from you, carefully holding all the strings taut with the single loop held between your right thumb and forefinger. As you do, the tent will take shape.

Middling Cradles

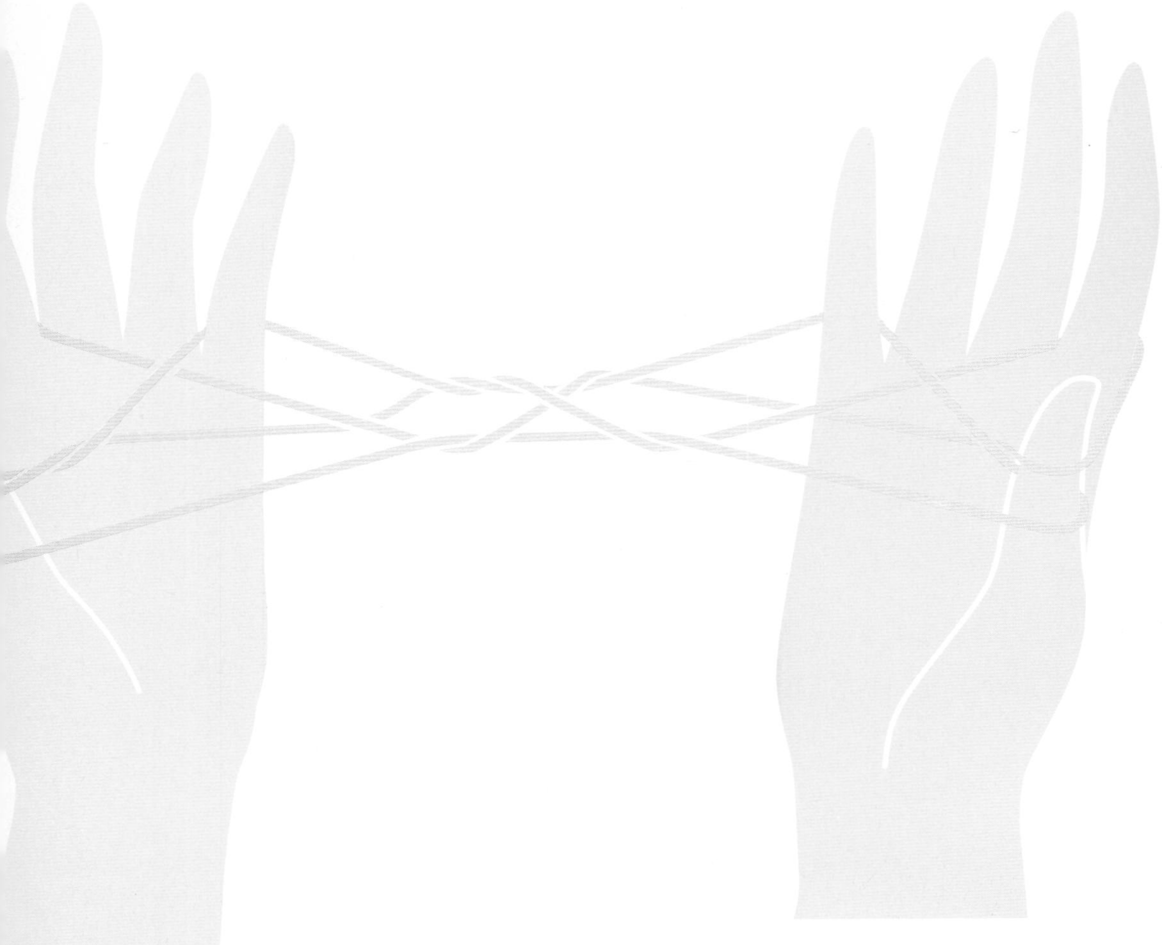

It's time to try something slightly harder.
These figures represent an intermediate stage
– every one of them has a tricky element or
two, although none of them will have you
tearing your hair out as you learn. You'll find
that cat's cradles can be deceptive, too: the
game that looks the simplest in this section
– the Torres Straits Lizard – is actually one
of the hardest to get right, while Jacob's
Ladder or the Caribou, both much tougher
options at first glance, are relatively
straightforward sequences provided that
you read the steps through carefully before
you start. Have fun and work on your skills,
because the next chapter will call on all the
dexterity you can muster.

Navajo Bow

Among the string figures collected together in the early part of the twentieth century were a number of games or sequences specific to various Native American tribes. Of the figures gathered by Caroline Furness Jayne, by far the largest share of these are attributed to the Navajo, with just a handful collected from the Apache and the Osage tribe. The three examples shown on the following pages – the Navajo Bow, Navajo Lightning and Navajo Stars – are fiddly but not really difficult. They all start in the same way but go in very different directions. Take careful note of which finger goes over and under each string, both in the instructions and the illustrations – mistakes can be hard to spot after they happen.

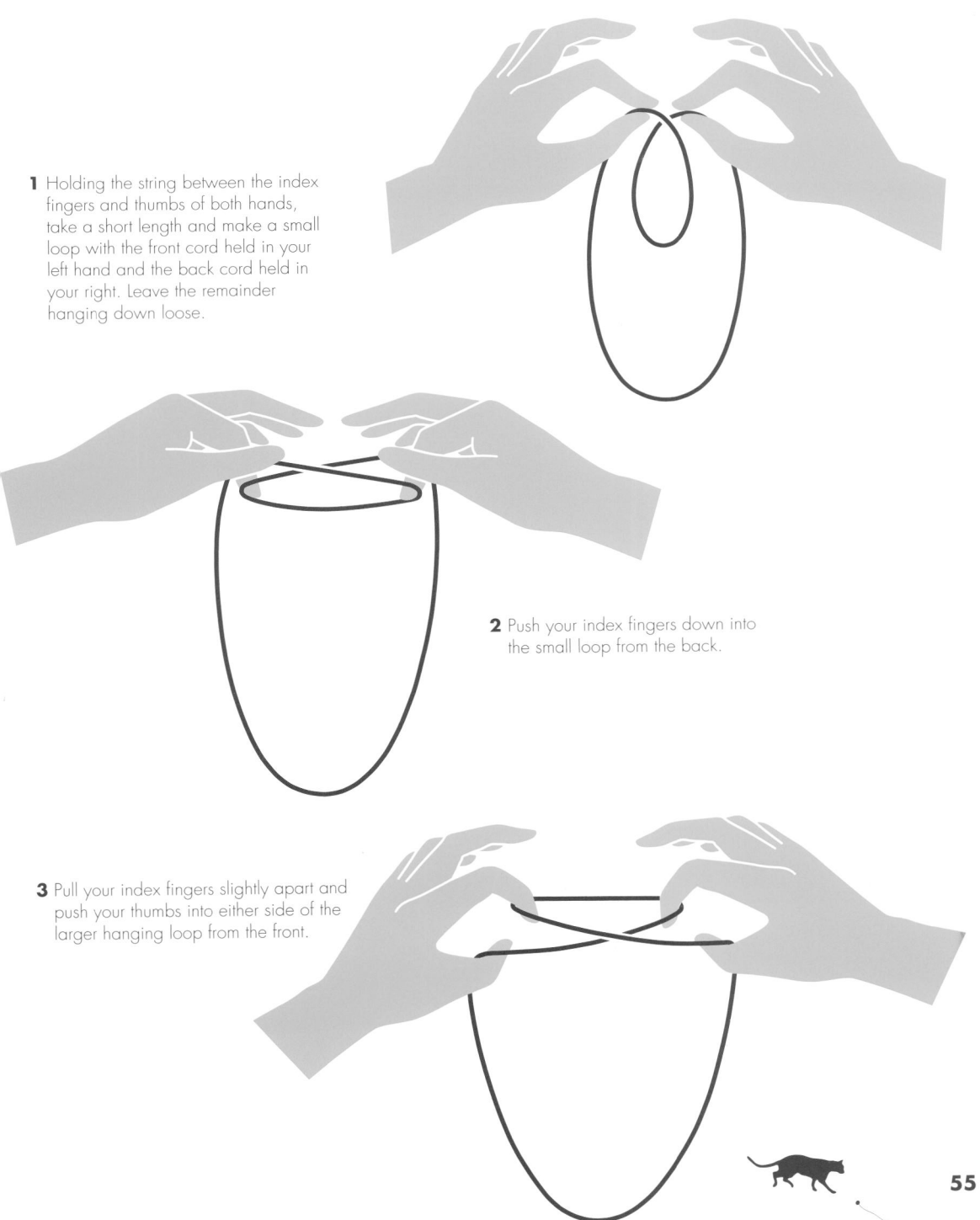

1 Holding the string between the index fingers and thumbs of both hands, take a short length and make a small loop with the front cord held in your left hand and the back cord held in your right. Leave the remainder hanging down loose.

2 Push your index fingers down into the small loop from the back.

3 Pull your index fingers slightly apart and push your thumbs into either side of the larger hanging loop from the front.

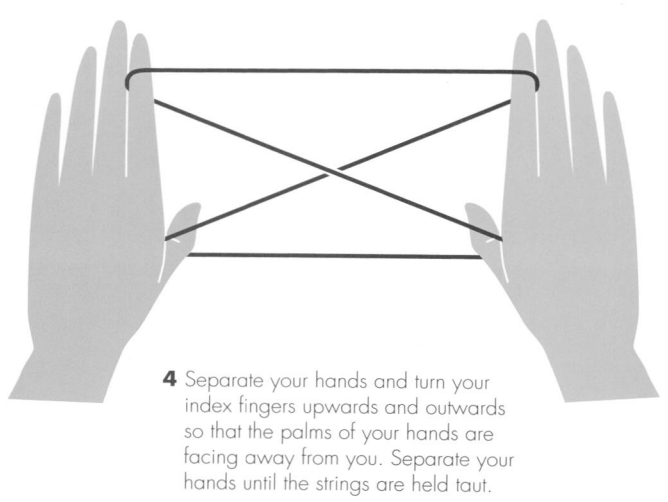

4 Separate your hands and turn your
index fingers upwards and outwards
so that the palms of your hands are
facing away from you. Separate your
hands until the strings are held taut.

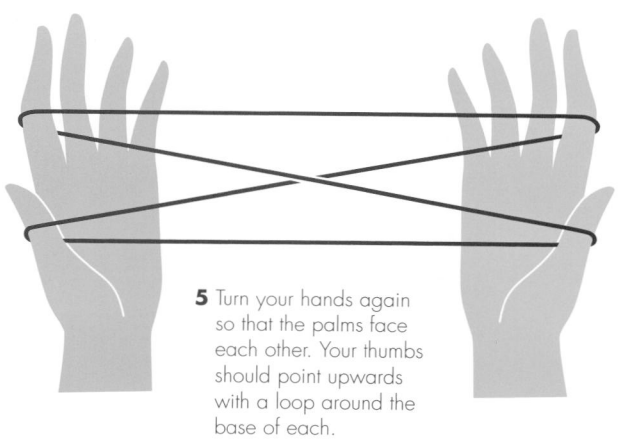

5 Turn your hands again
so that the palms face
each other. Your thumbs
should point upwards
with a loop around the
base of each.

6 Place your thumbs over the near index string and under
the far index string then return them to their previous
position, bringing the far index string back with them.

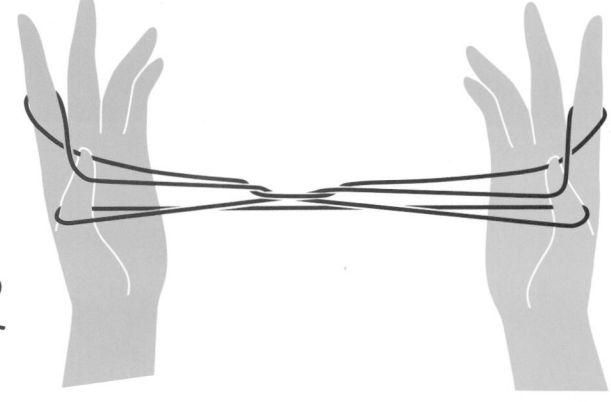

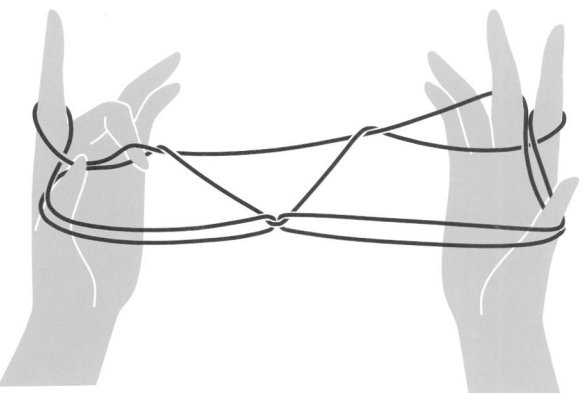

7 Bring your middle fingers towards you over the near index string and under the far thumb string, then return them to their previous position, taking the far thumb string with them.

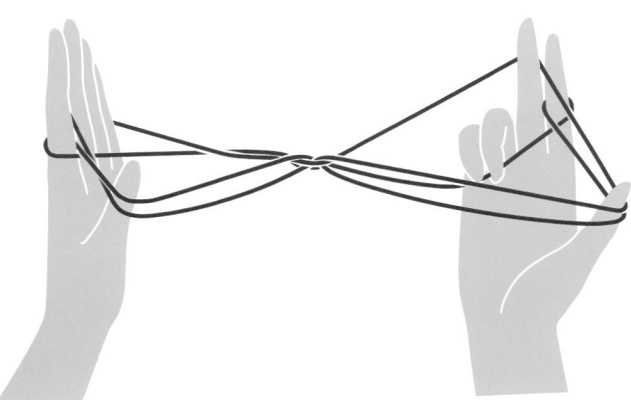

8 Turn your palms towards you and push the ring and little fingers of both hands up between the near index string and the far middle-finger string (this is getting complicated!), then pull down the near index string by touching the ring and little fingertips of both hands on your palms (shown in the position of the right hand in the illustration).

9 Almost there…Holding the middle and index fingers of both hands upright, slip the loops off your thumbs and turn the palms of your hands away from you, pulling them apart as you do and revealing the completed Bow. Be careful not to lose hold of the strings held against your palms in this last step.

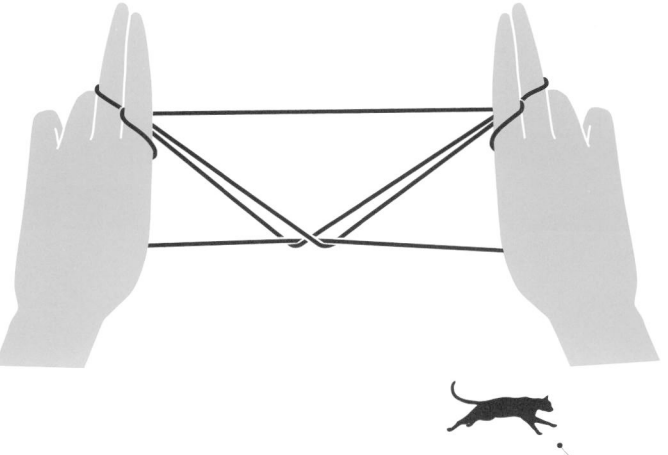

Navajo Stars

This is the simplest of the figures in this collection that use the Navajo Bow opening, and a good 'cradle' to turn to for light relief if the complex moves of the Bow and Navajo Lightning are eluding you. While far from the simplest string figure in this book (it's still quite fiddly to do), you'll probably find that you can complete this one successfully after one or two practice runs.

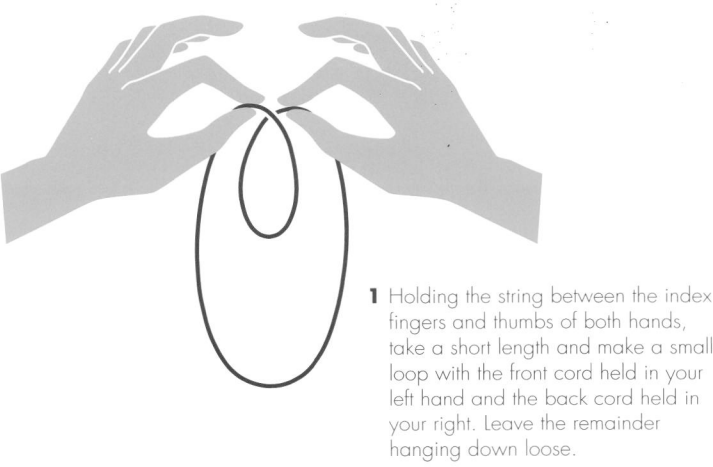

1 Holding the string between the index
   fingers and thumbs of both hands,
   take a short length and make a small
   loop with the front cord held in your
   left hand and the back cord held in
   your right. Leave the remainder
   hanging down loose.

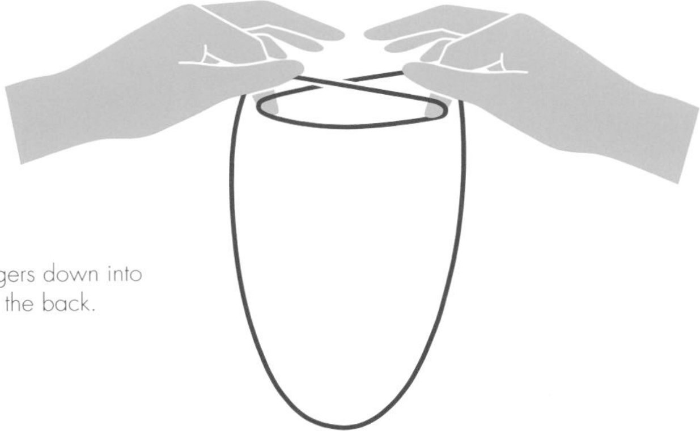

2 Push your index fingers down into
   the small loop from the back.

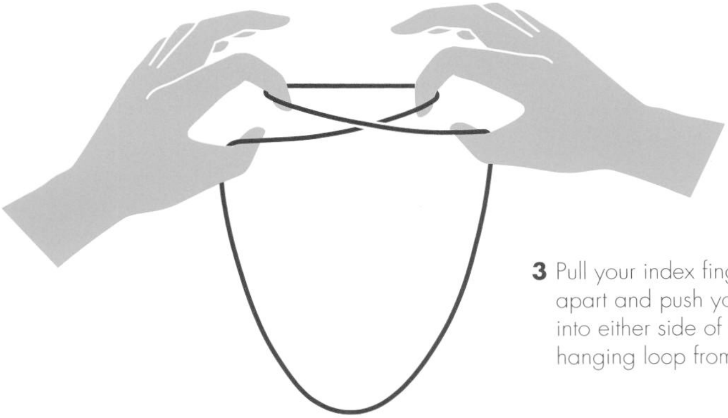

3 Pull your index fingers slightly
   apart and push your thumbs
   into either side of the larger
   hanging loop from the front.

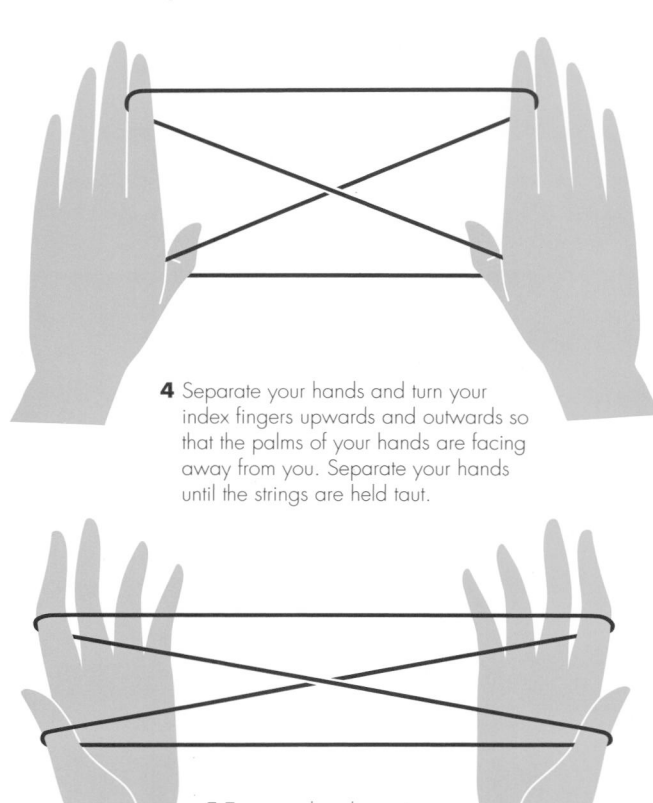

4 Separate your hands and turn your index fingers upwards and outwards so that the palms of your hands are facing away from you. Separate your hands until the strings are held taut.

5 Turn your hands again so that the palms face each other. Your thumbs should point upwards with a loop around the base of each.

6 Push your thumbs up into the loops on your index fingers from below, then slip your index fingers out of the loops so that they are transferred completely to your thumbs. There will now be two loops around each thumb – keep the second as close to the tops of your thumbs as you can without allowing it to slip off.

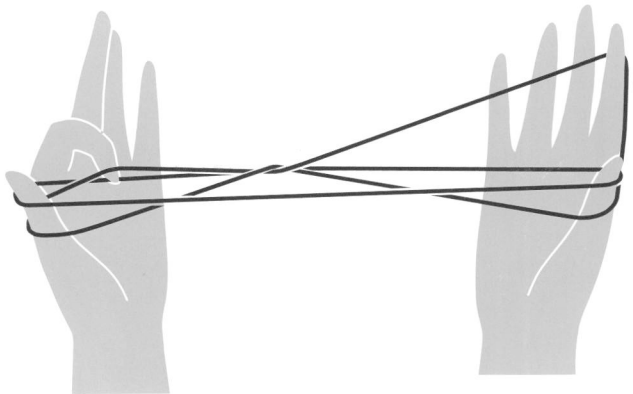

7 Place your index fingers over the far upper thumb string and catch the lower thumb strings furthest from you (shown on the left hand in the illustration). Straighten your index fingers so that the string is lifted up on the back of each index finger (shown on the right hand in the illustration).

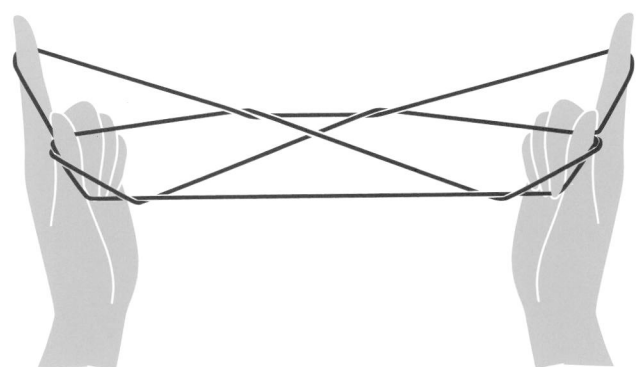

8 Pair your middle and ring fingers and push them towards you, through each of the lower loops on your thumbs from below. Catch the upper thumb string nearest you between them.

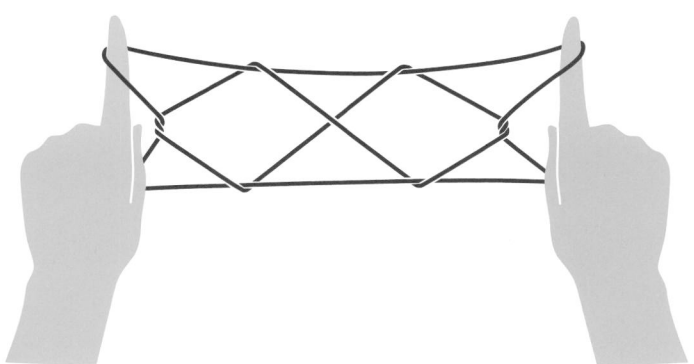

9 Draw the upper thumb string away from you through the lower thumb loops, then hook your middle fingers over it. At the same time slip the loops off your thumbs and turn your hands away from you, index fingers held straight out. The strings around your index fingers and held to your palms by your middle fingers will tauten, completing the Navajo Stars pattern.

Navajo Lightning

Navajo Lightning is the hardest of this sequence of three Native American figures, and it may take a number of sessions before you're able to complete the last three steps. It's worth it – the tangled strings look like a mess just before the final stage but, managed correctly, miraculously turn into a neat forked-lightning shape in the very last move. It's easy to let complex looping slip off your fingers when you don't mean to, so do be patient and read the steps very carefully as you go. If you start to feel frustrated, do one or two easy figures and come back to this one later.

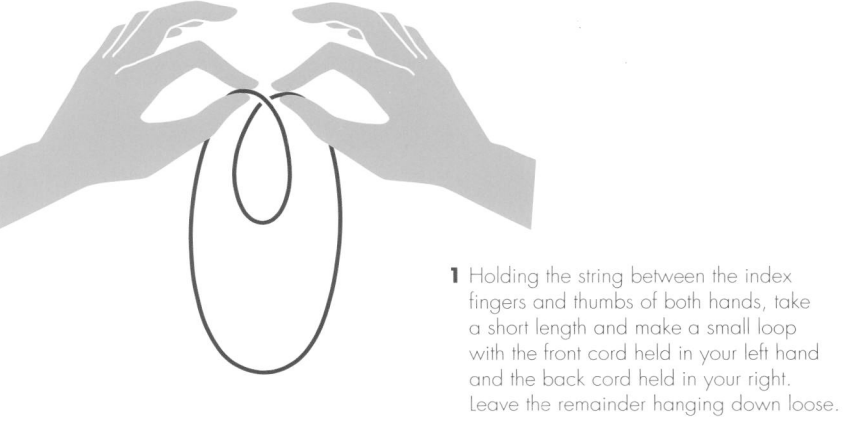

1 Holding the string between the index
fingers and thumbs of both hands, take
a short length and make a small loop
with the front cord held in your left hand
and the back cord held in your right.
Leave the remainder hanging down loose.

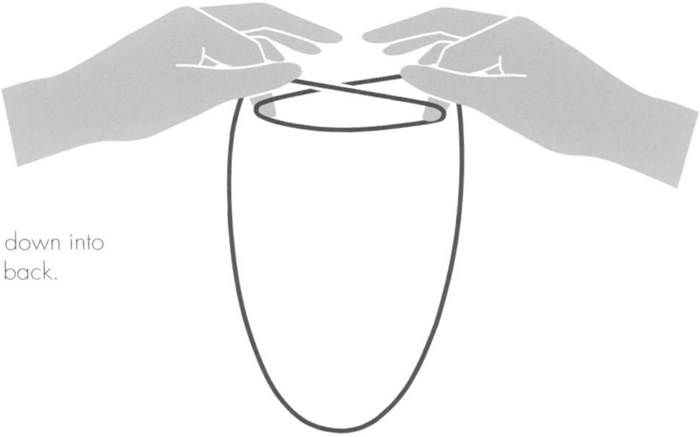

2 Push your index fingers down into
the small loop from the back.

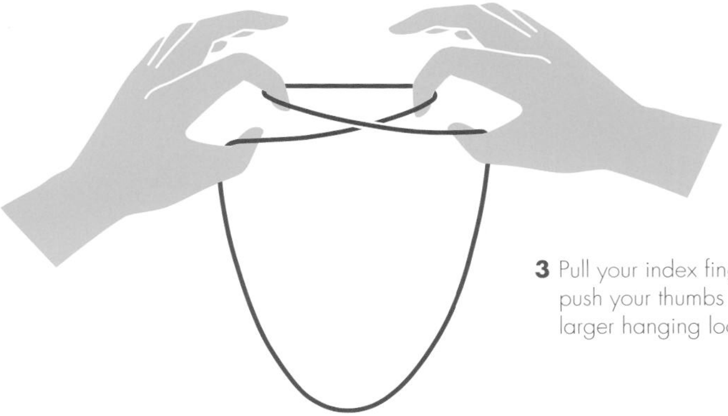

3 Pull your index fingers slightly apart and
push your thumbs into either side of the
larger hanging loop from the front.

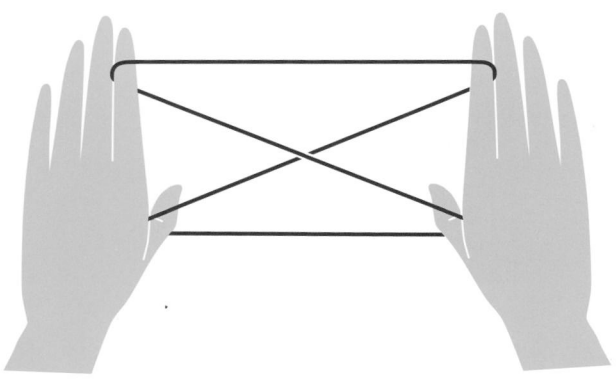

4 Separate your hands and
turn your index fingers
upwards and outwards so
that the palms of your hands
are facing away from you.
Separate your hands until
the strings are held taut.

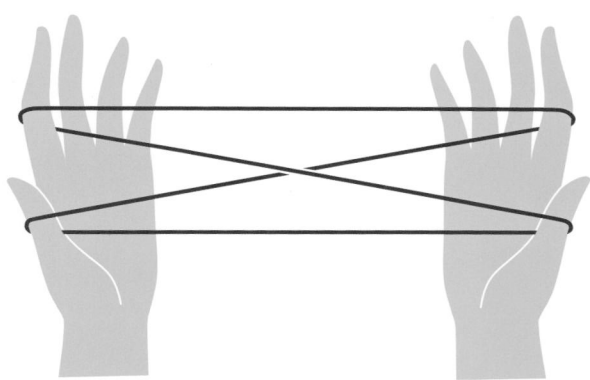

5 Turn your hands again
so that the palms face
each other. Your thumbs
should point upwards
with a loop around the
base of each.

6 Place your thumbs over the
near index string and under
the far index string, then
return them to their previous
position, bringing the far
index string back with them.

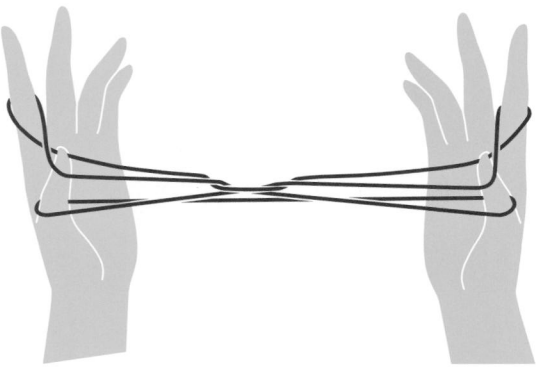

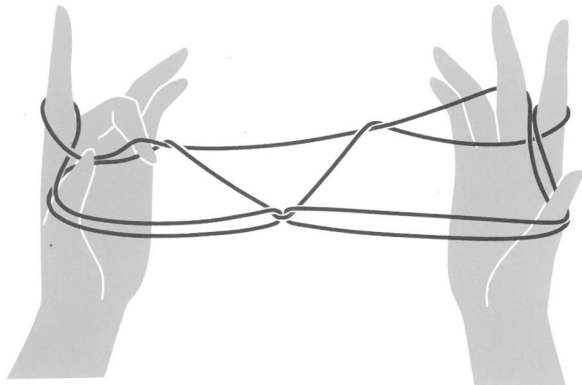

7 Bring your middle fingers towards you over the near index string and under the far thumb string, then return them to their previous position, taking the far thumb string with them.

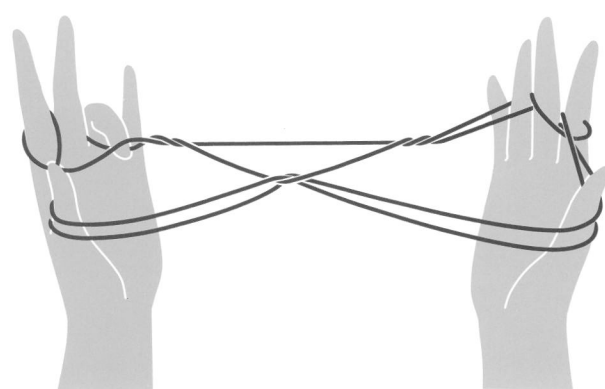

8 Bring your ring fingers towards you over the far middle-finger string and under the near index-finger string (seen on the left hand in the illustration) then return them to their original position, carrying the near index-finger string on the back of each ring finger as you do so (seen on the right hand in the illustration). You may find this step easier if you do it one hand at a time.

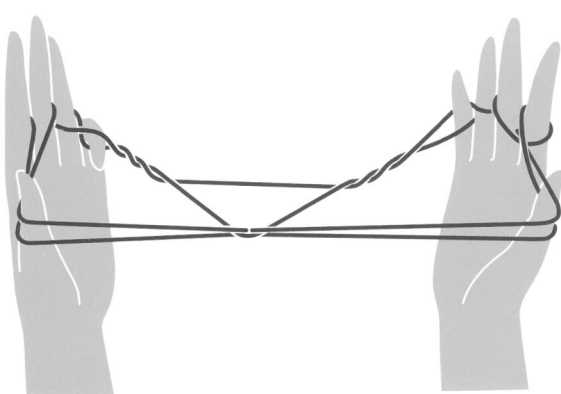

9 Bring your little fingers towards you, taking them over the far ring-finger string and taking up the far middle-finger string on the back of them from below (seen on the left hand in the illustration) then return your little fingers to their original position (seen on the right hand in the illustration). At the end of this tricky step you have two twisted strings leading from your little fingers, two straight strings looped around each of your thumbs and two strings laced between your other fingers. Check the illustration carefully before carrying on to the final steps.

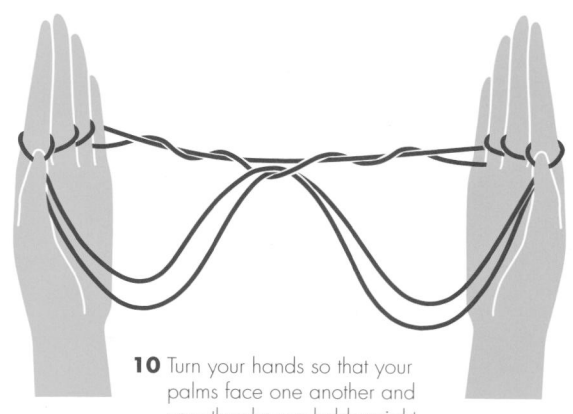

10 Turn your hands so that your palms face one another and your thumbs are held upright, then carefully slip your thumbs out of their loops. Hold the rest of your fingers closely together as you do so to avoid any of the other loops slipping off.

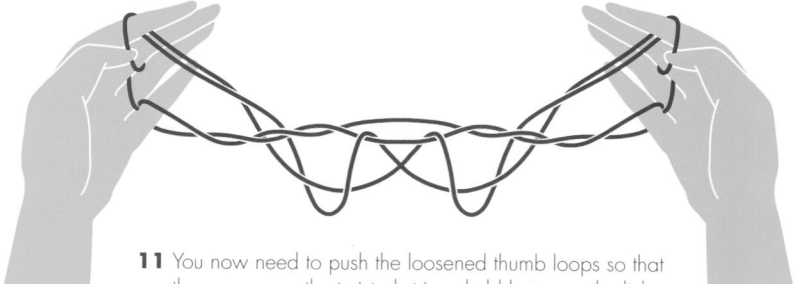

11 You now need to push the loosened thumb loops so that they pass over the twisted strings held between the little fingers and hang down behind them. It's easiest to ask a friend to take them gently and position them for you, otherwise it's difficult to manage the 'throwover' without some of the other loops slipping out of position.

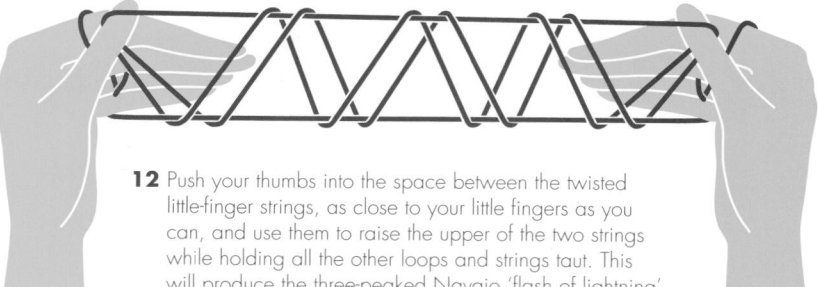

12 Push your thumbs into the space between the twisted little-finger strings, as close to your little fingers as you can, and use them to raise the upper of the two strings while holding all the other loops and strings taut. This will produce the three-peaked Navajo 'flash of lightning'.

The Torres Straits Lizard

This figure is harder to master than it looks. It's the type of game in which you first create an apparently tight string 'trap' (in this case around your right wrist), which is undone at the end with a single slick movement. It's definitely one to try out a few times before showing it off to friends. Read the steps and look at the pictures carefully as you learn; although it's short and apparently simple there are more ways to go wrong than you'd think. It was first illustrated in Jayne's book in 1906, where she names it the Torres Straits Lizard, the figure having originated on the islands of the Torres Strait, although she also notes that in at least one of the islands the same figure is called Intestines of a Turtle. Quite why it has either name is a mystery – perhaps the wrist-catch is the bite of the lizard?

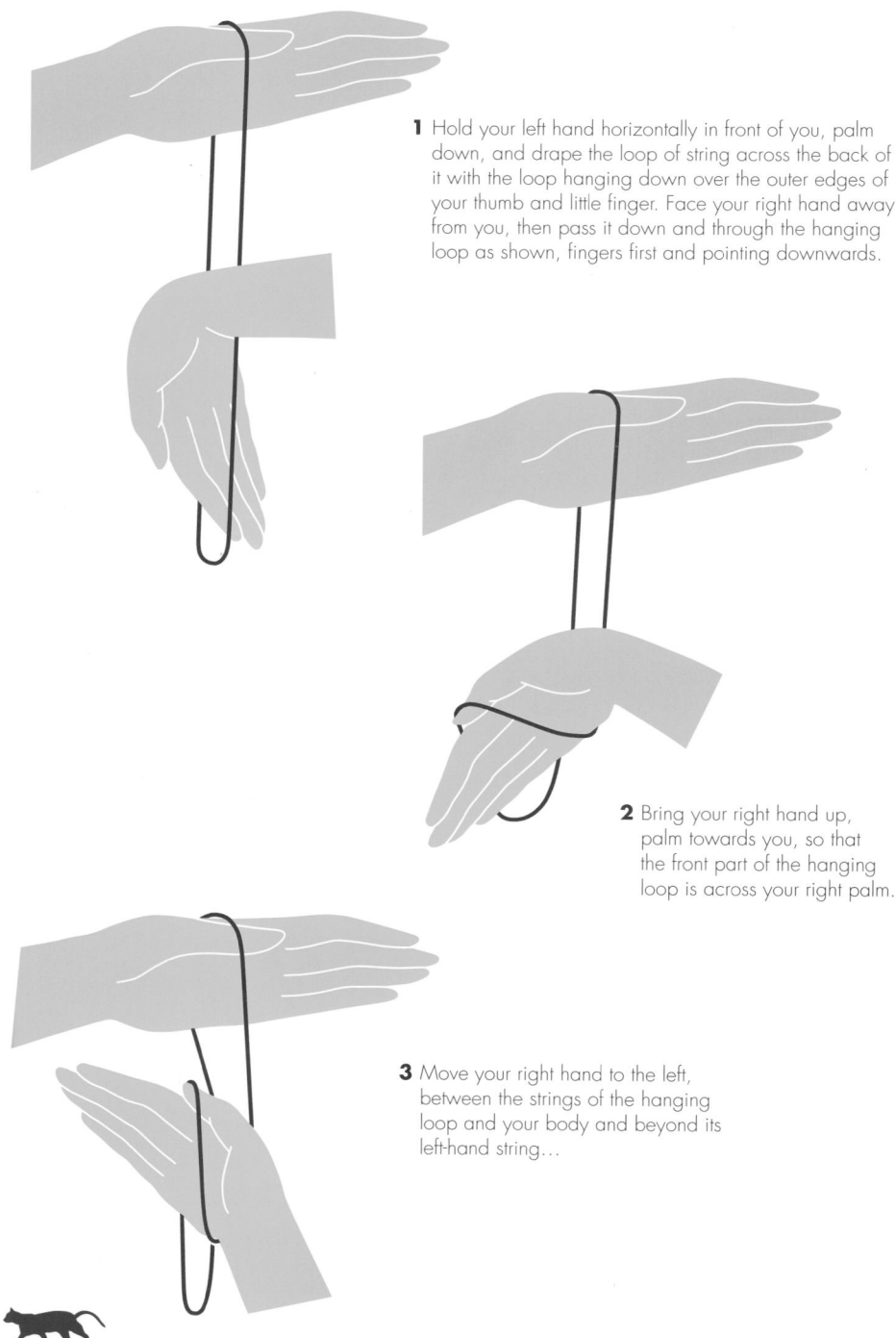

1 Hold your left hand horizontally in front of you, palm down, and drape the loop of string across the back of it with the loop hanging down over the outer edges of your thumb and little finger. Face your right hand away from you, then pass it down and through the hanging loop as shown, fingers first and pointing downwards.

2 Bring your right hand up, palm towards you, so that the front part of the hanging loop is across your right palm.

3 Move your right hand to the left, between the strings of the hanging loop and your body and beyond its left-hand string…

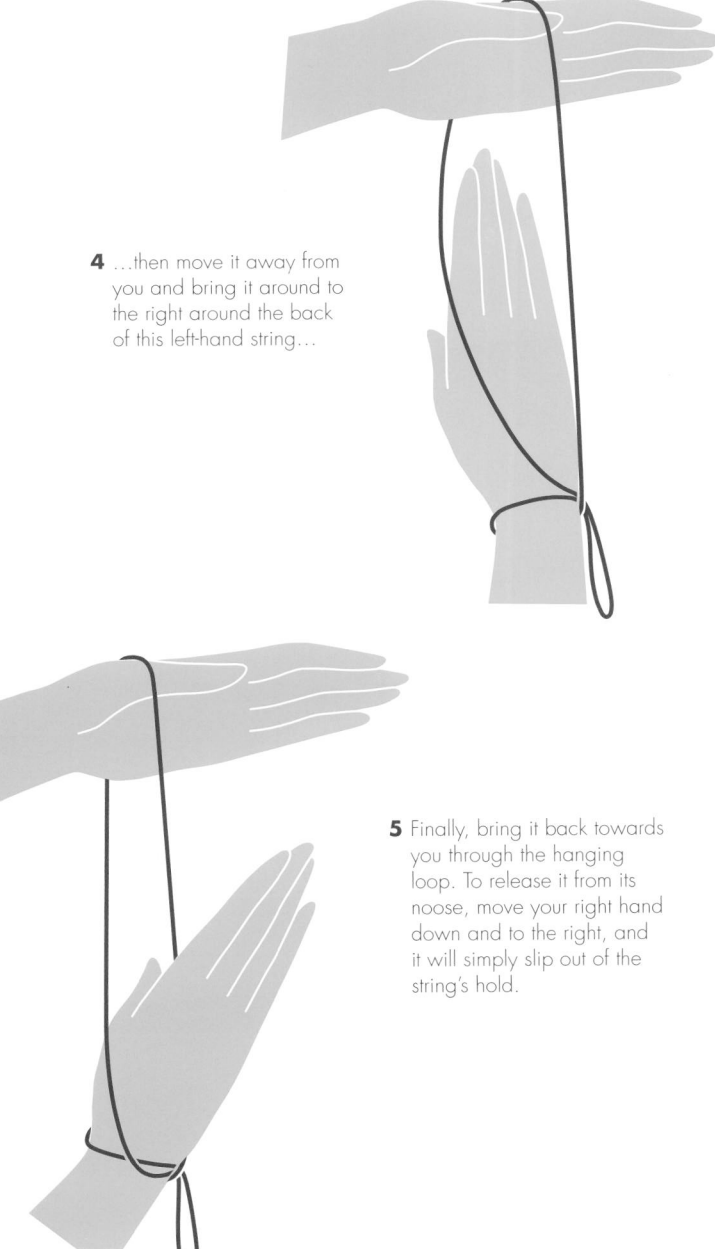

4 ...then move it away from you and bring it around to the right around the back of this left-hand string...

5 Finally, bring it back towards you through the hanging loop. To release it from its noose, move your right hand down and to the right, and it will simply slip out of the string's hold.

Jacob's Ladder

This is one of the great classic string games, and it exists
in different incarnations in many different cultures. In North
America it's known as Osage Diamonds after the Osage tribe
among whom it is believed to have originated, while some
Oceanic peoples call it the Fishing Net. It was first collected in
Caroline Furness Jayne's *String Figures and How to Make Them*.
Whatever its name, the final stages of this 'cradle' (from Step 10
onwards) are quite tricky to manage. Keep practising: you may
need a few tries before all the moves fall into place and you can
manage it as a fluid sequence.

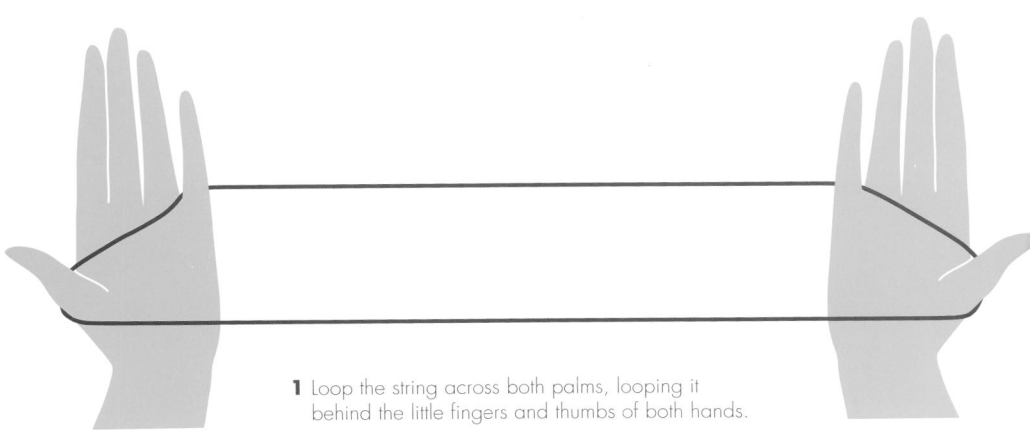

1 Loop the string across both palms, looping it behind the little fingers and thumbs of both hands.

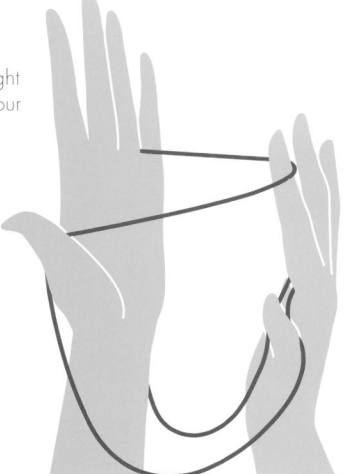

2 Place the index finger of your right hand under the palm string of your left and pull your hands apart.

3 Repeat on the other side, placing the index finger of your left hand under the palm string of your right.

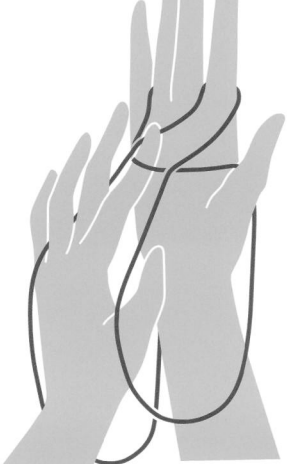

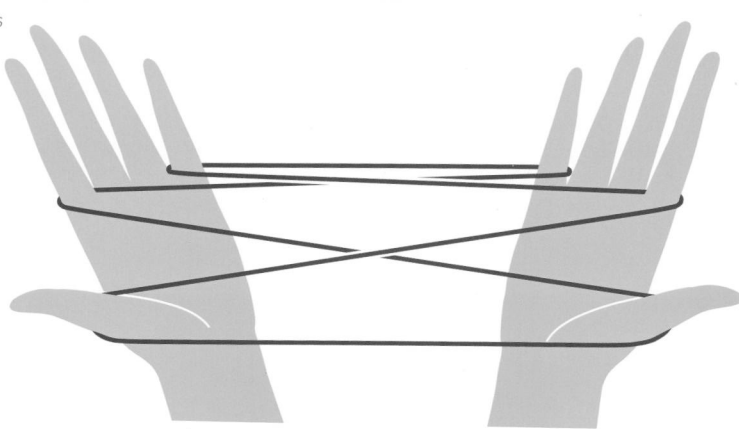

4 Pull your hands apart; you'll have loops of string around both little fingers, index fingers and thumbs.

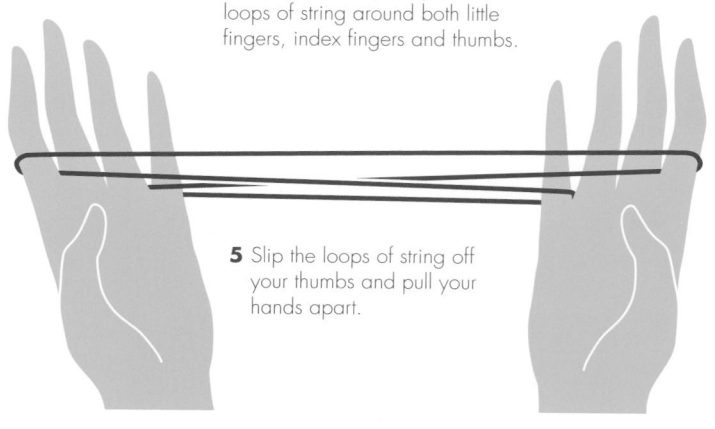

5 Slip the loops of string off your thumbs and pull your hands apart.

6 Move your thumbs forward, under all the strings, and hook them backwards over the furthest string (the outer one around the little finger) and bring it back over your thumbs as you return them to their original position.

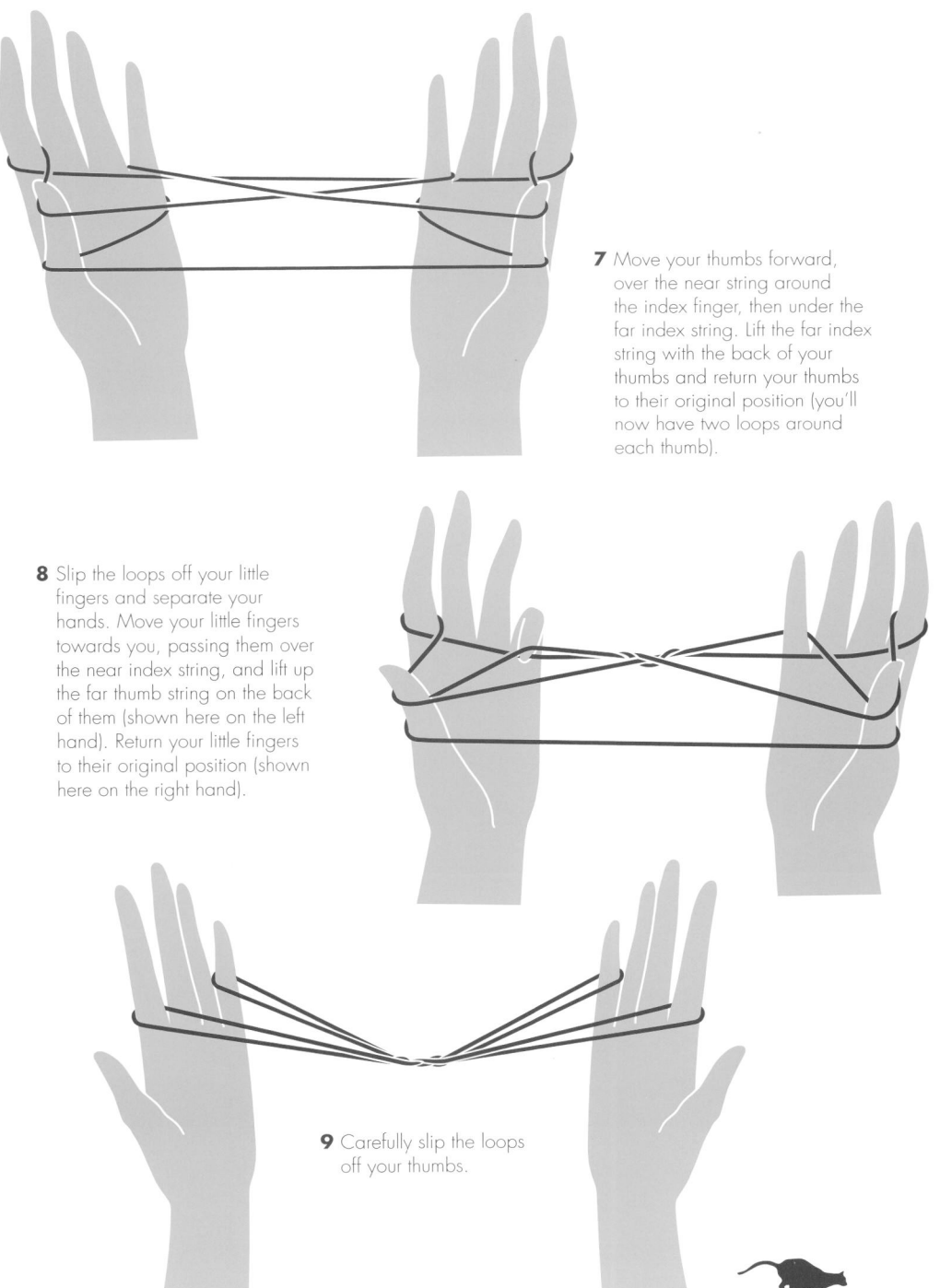

7 Move your thumbs forward, over the near string around the index finger, then under the far index string. Lift the far index string with the back of your thumbs and return your thumbs to their original position (you'll now have two loops around each thumb).

8 Slip the loops off your little fingers and separate your hands. Move your little fingers towards you, passing them over the near index string, and lift up the far thumb string on the back of them (shown here on the left hand). Return your little fingers to their original position (shown here on the right hand).

9 Carefully slip the loops off your thumbs.

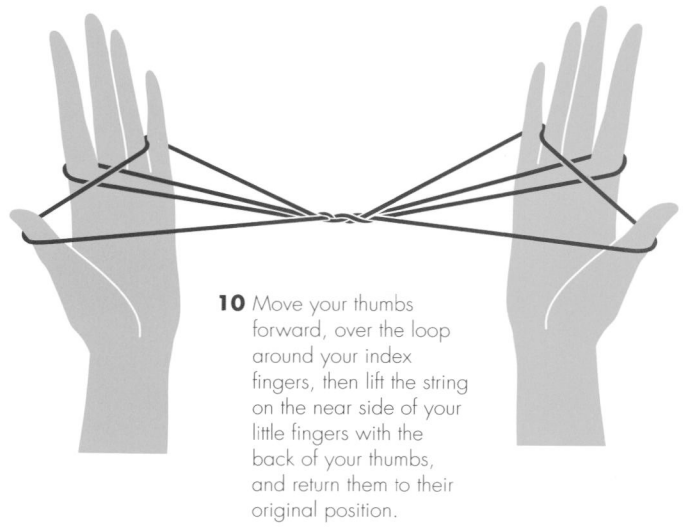

10 Move your thumbs forward, over the loop around your index fingers, then lift the string on the near side of your little fingers with the back of your thumbs, and return them to their original position.

11 Use your right thumb and index finger to pick up the closest left index-finger string and slip it over your left thumb. Then repeat, using the left thumb and index finger to slip the closest right index-finger string over your right thumb. (This step can be tricky at first and may take a few tries to get right. If it doesn't go smoothly, take a deep breath, count to ten and start again.)

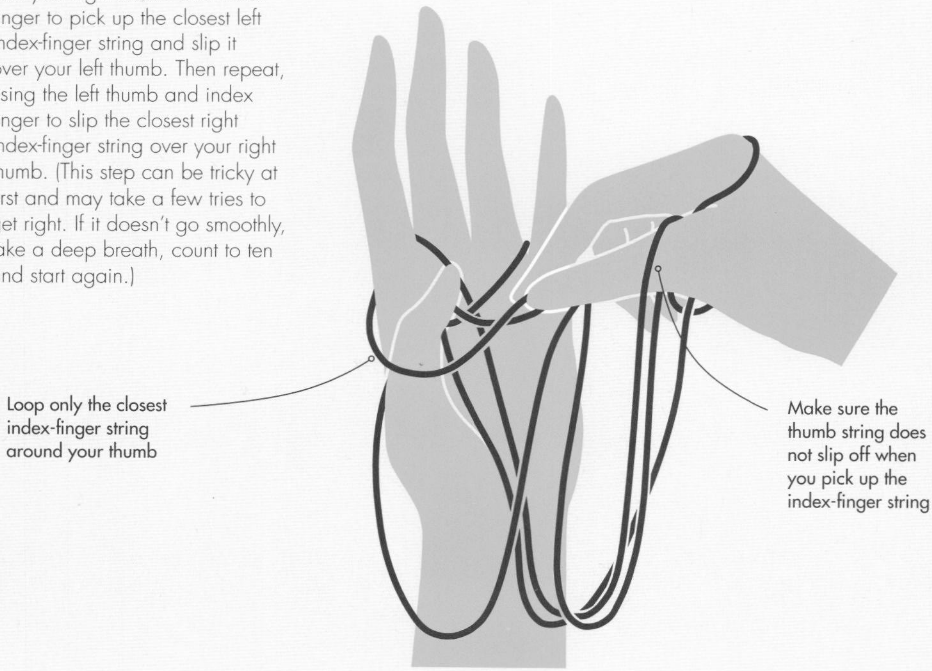

Loop only the closest index-finger string around your thumb

Make sure the thumb string does not slip off when you pick up the index-finger string

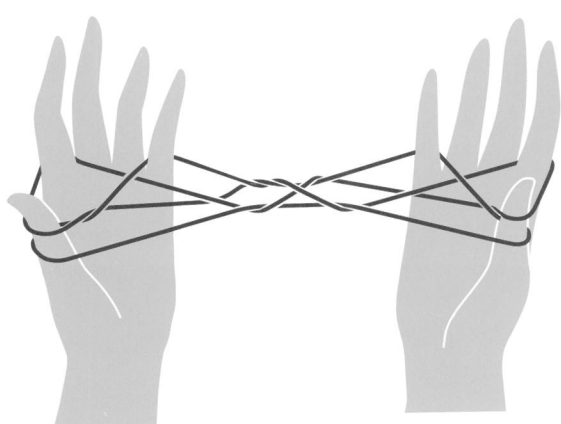

12 When both the loops are securely over your thumbs, gently pull your hands apart.

13 Now you need to slip the lower loop off each thumb but without disturbing the upper one. Bend your left thumb towards your other hand and then up towards you to slip it off easily (shown on the left hand in this illustration). Repeat with the right thumb. Push your index fingers downwards into the small triangle formed by the string twisted around the thumb loops.

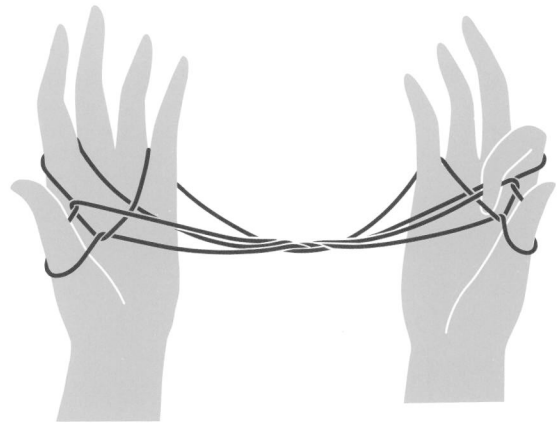

14 Turn the palms of both hands downwards and away from you and, as you do so, drop the loops from your little fingers. Pull your hands gently apart, and you've completed Jacob's Ladder.

Two-man Diamonds

This is one of the patterns that result in a netted shape, but it differs from some other nets in this book in that it calls for a second player to support the later steps while you organize the strings. There are two tricky elements: it's hard at some points to keep the loops from slipping off the tips of your thumbs, and the slipping on and off of the strings between your wrists and your fingers can be less than smooth on your first couple of attempts. Jayne features this figure in her classic collection, where she dubs it Pygmy Diamonds, recalling first seeing it demonstrated by a member of a Congolese pygmy tribe at the St Louis Exposition of 1884.

1 Put both your hands through the string loop so that it's around your wrists. Using both thumbs and index fingers, make a small loop from the string nearest to you. The string of the loop should pass from left to right, as shown.

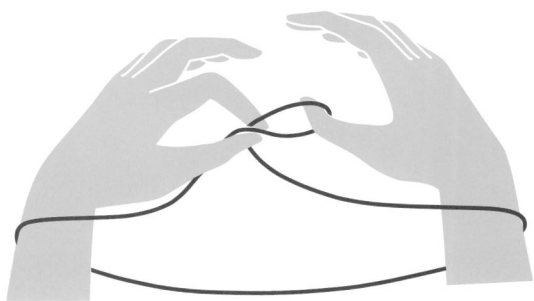

2 Put your right thumb through this smaller ring from the front, pulling it up as you do so.

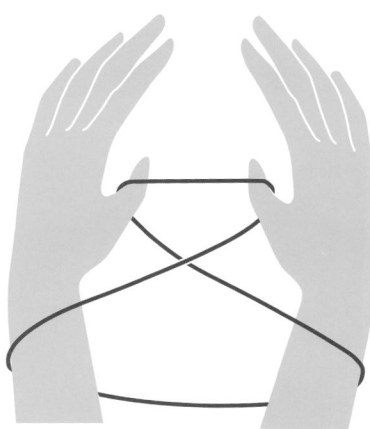

3 Repeat with your left thumb so that the string is around both wrists and both thumbs.

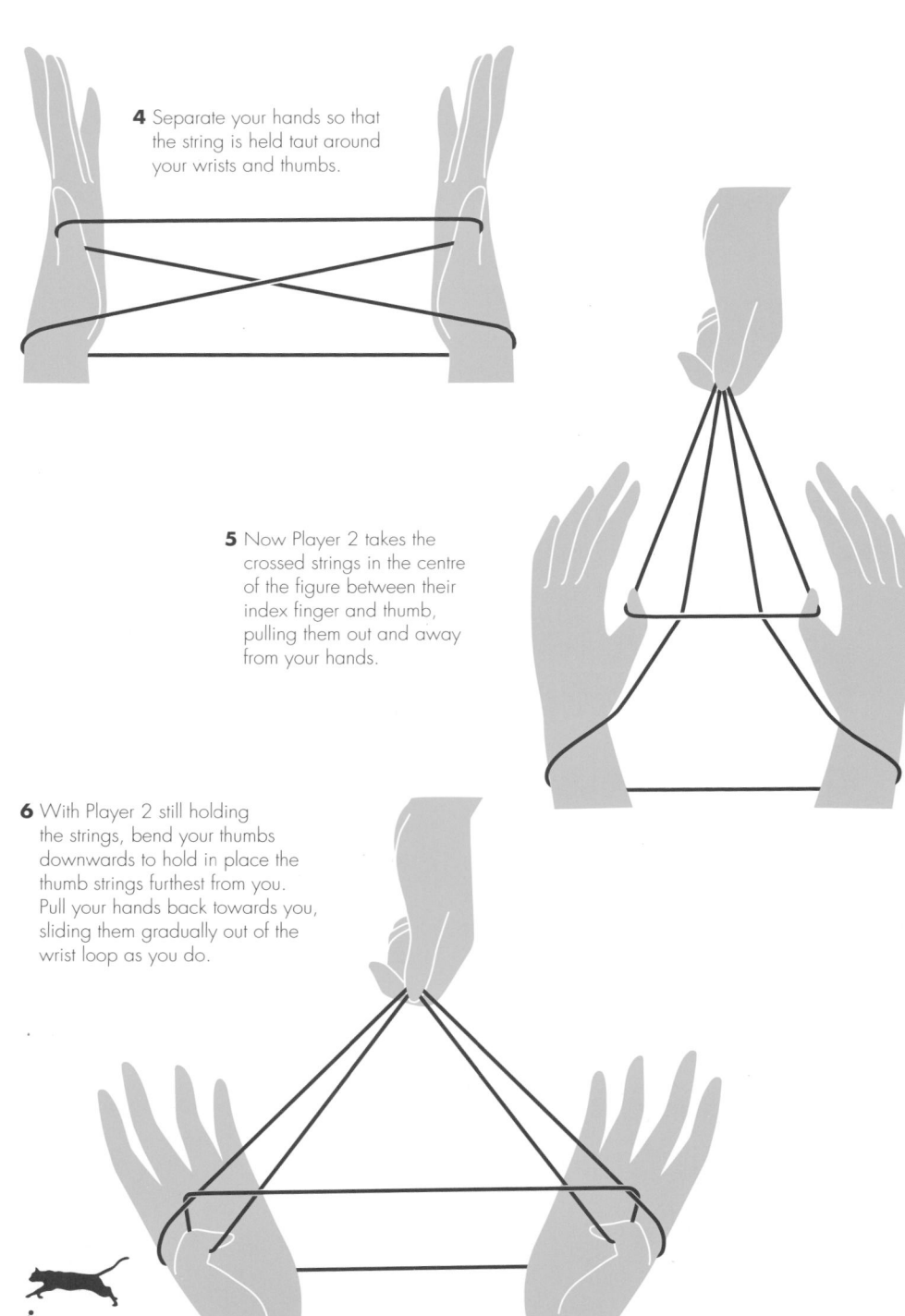

4 Separate your hands so that the string is held taut around your wrists and thumbs.

5 Now Player 2 takes the crossed strings in the centre of the figure between their index finger and thumb, pulling them out and away from your hands.

6 With Player 2 still holding the strings, bend your thumbs downwards to hold in place the thumb strings furthest from you. Pull your hands back towards you, sliding them gradually out of the wrist loop as you do.

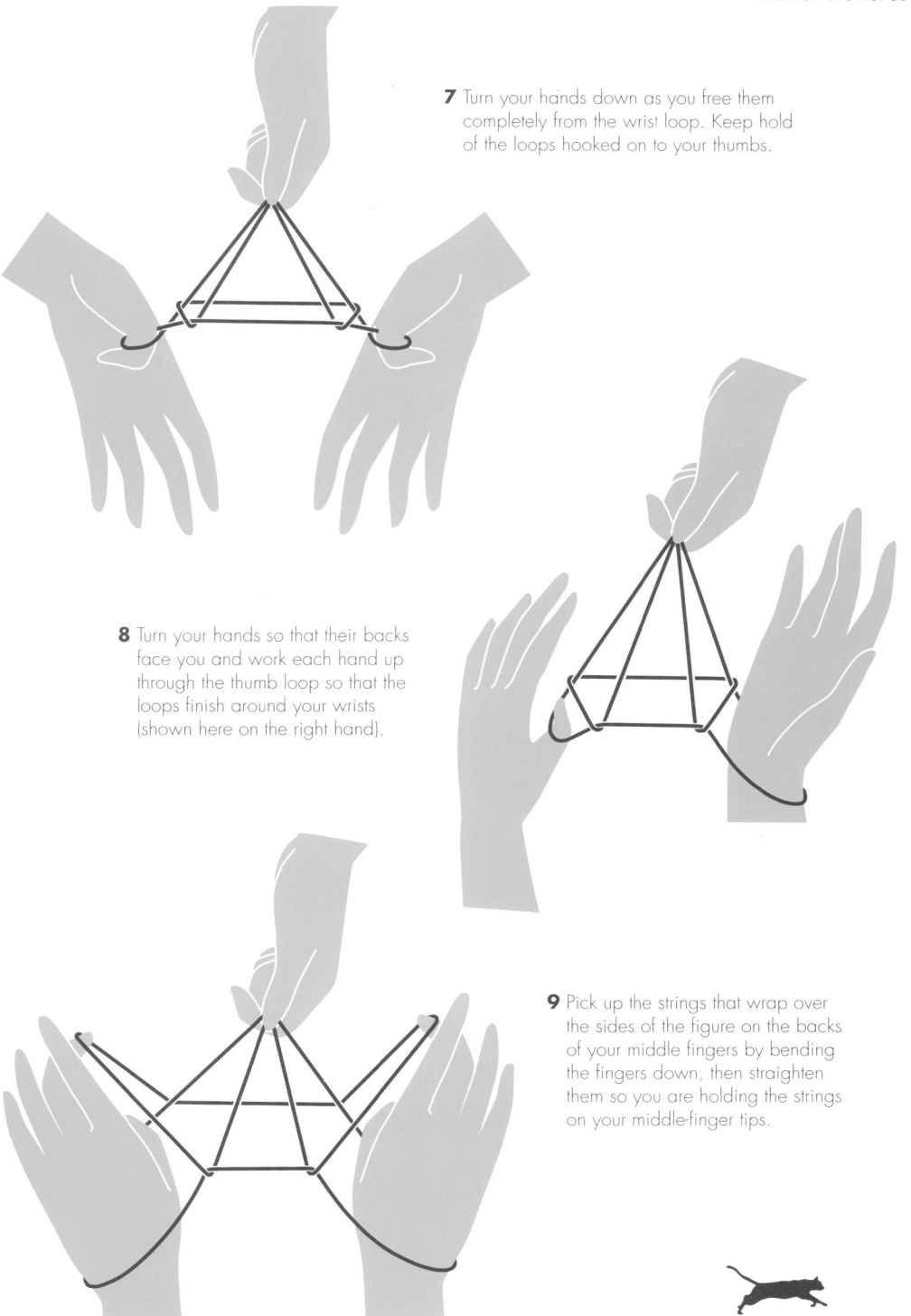

7 Turn your hands down as you free them completely from the wrist loop. Keep hold of the loops hooked on to your thumbs.

8 Turn your hands so that their backs face you and work each hand up through the thumb loop so that the loops finish around your wrists (shown here on the right hand).

9 Pick up the strings that wrap over the sides of the figure on the backs of your middle fingers by bending the fingers down, then straighten them so you are holding the strings on your middle-finger tips.

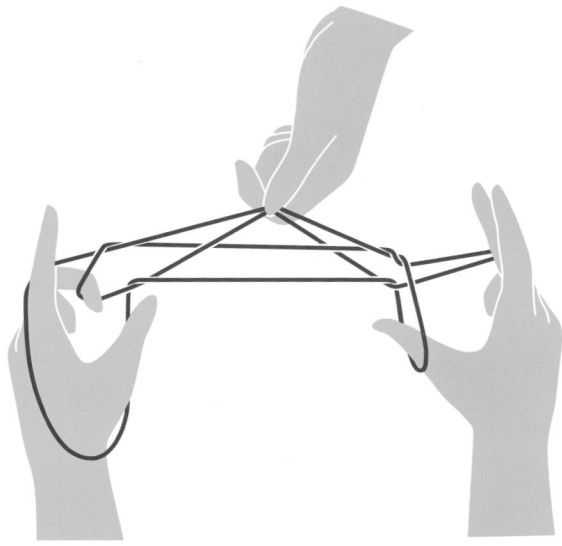

10 Turn your palms back towards you slightly and hook your middle fingers over the middle-finger strings nearest to you. Keep these strings hooked by your middle fingers while working your wrists back through the wrist loops, catching them on the back of your thumbs as they loosen (shown here on the left hand). Turn your hands palms towards you and pull the loops on your middle fingers further through the thumb loops. Turn your palms slightly upwards and straighten your middle fingers outside the thumb loops (shown here on the right hand).

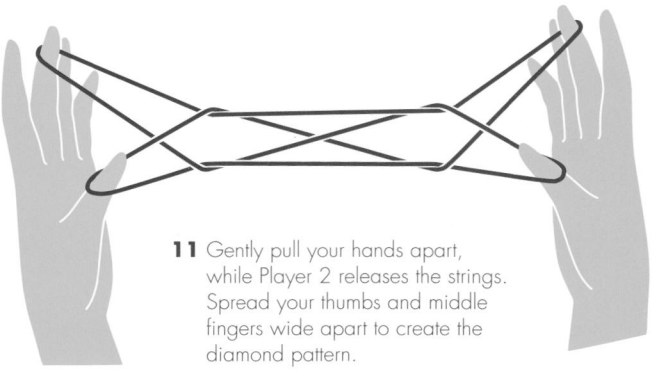

11 Gently pull your hands apart, while Player 2 releases the strings. Spread your thumbs and middle fingers wide apart to create the diamond pattern.

The Caribou

String figures don't always look much like their names, but
the final 'picture' in the Caribou sequence does, with a little
imagination, bear a distinct resemblance to a horned beast.
It was first collected from an Inuit tribe on Baffin Island, where
the migration of huge herds of caribou is still an annual sight,
so it's easy to see where its creators found their inspiration.
You'll find the middle steps of the sequence easier to manage if
you keep the strings on the right hand fairly near your fingertips,
while being careful that they don't slip off.

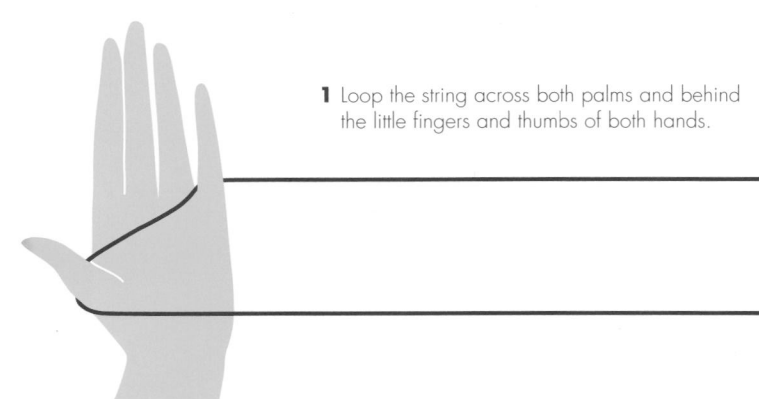
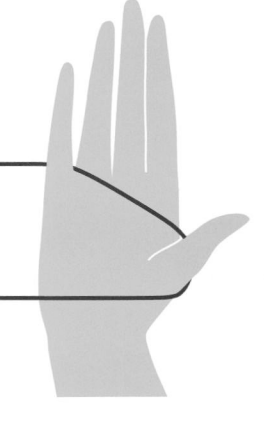

1 Loop the string across both palms and behind the little fingers and thumbs of both hands.

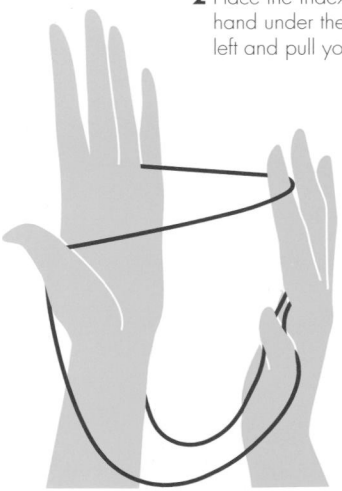

2 Place the index finger of your right hand under the palm string of your left and pull your hands apart.

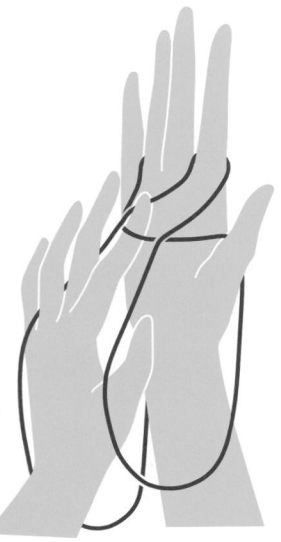

3 Repeat on the other side, placing the index finger of your left hand under the palm string of your right.

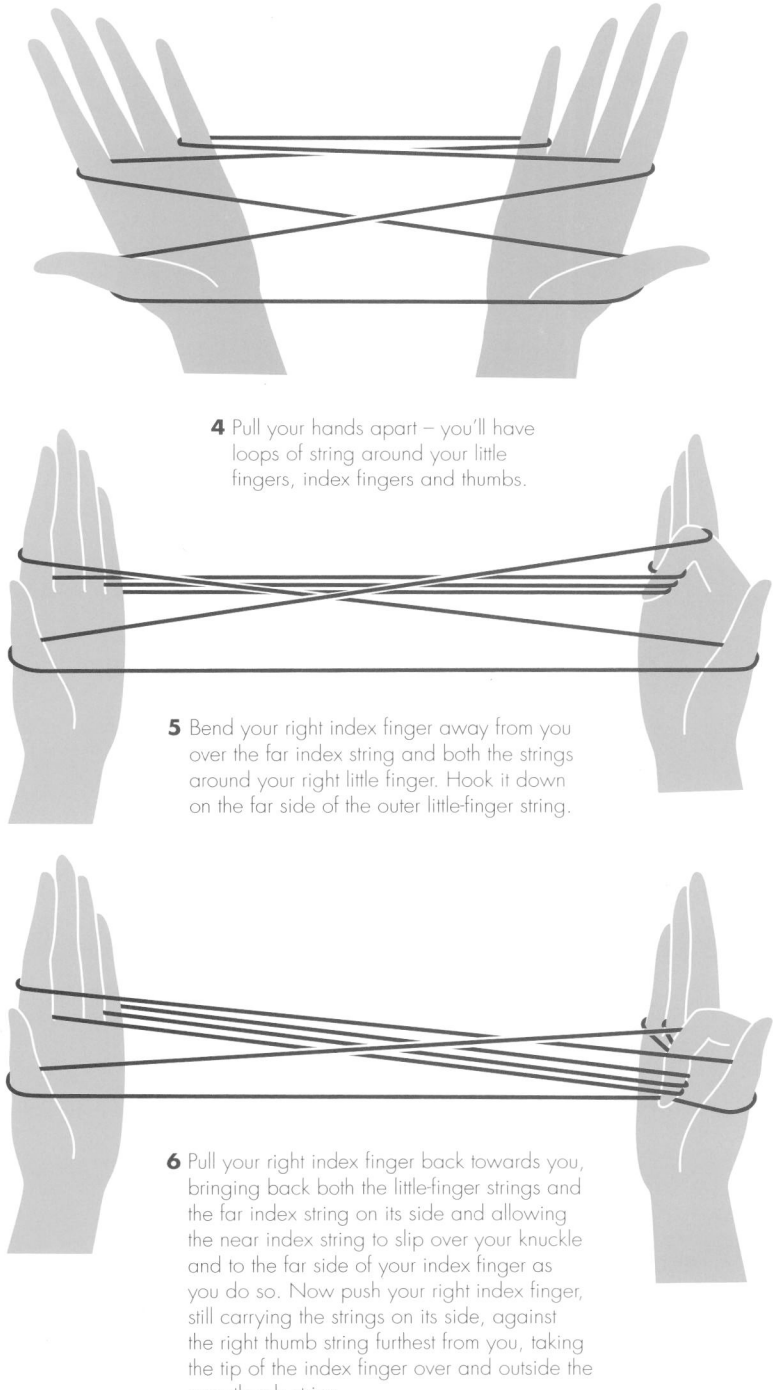

4 Pull your hands apart – you'll have loops of string around your little fingers, index fingers and thumbs.

5 Bend your right index finger away from you over the far index string and both the strings around your right little finger. Hook it down on the far side of the outer little-finger string.

6 Pull your right index finger back towards you, bringing back both the little-finger strings and the far index string on its side and allowing the near index string to slip over your knuckle and to the far side of your index finger as you do so. Now push your right index finger, still carrying the strings on its side, against the right thumb string furthest from you, taking the tip of the index finger over and outside the near thumb string

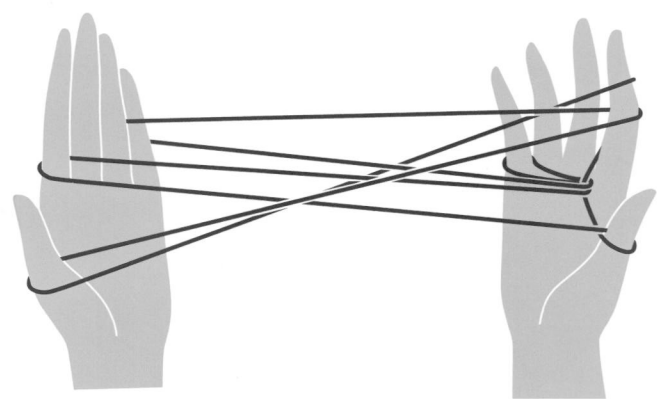

7 This next manoeuvre is the trickiest in the figure. Pick up the nearer thumb string with the far side of your bent right index finger and lift it up, along with the near index string, by swivelling your index finger away from you into its original upright position.

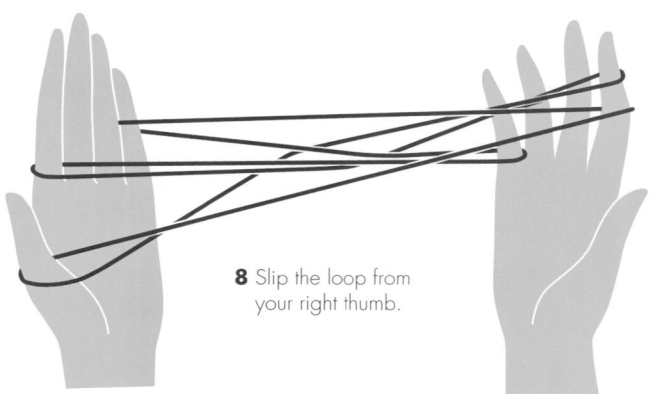

8 Slip the loop from your right thumb.

9 Twist the two loops on the right index finger by giving your finger a single full turn away from you. Push your right thumb up into the loops on your right index finger from beneath and pull the thumb outwards to make these loops larger. Use your left thumb and index finger to lift the loop from your left index finger and thread it through the two enlarged loops on your right index finger from above.

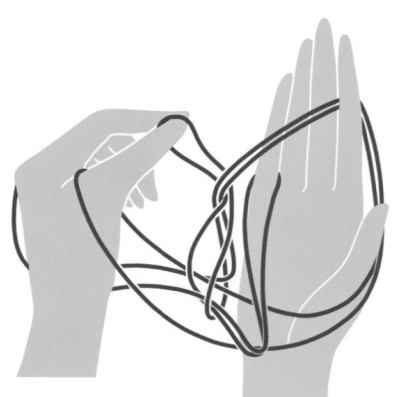

84

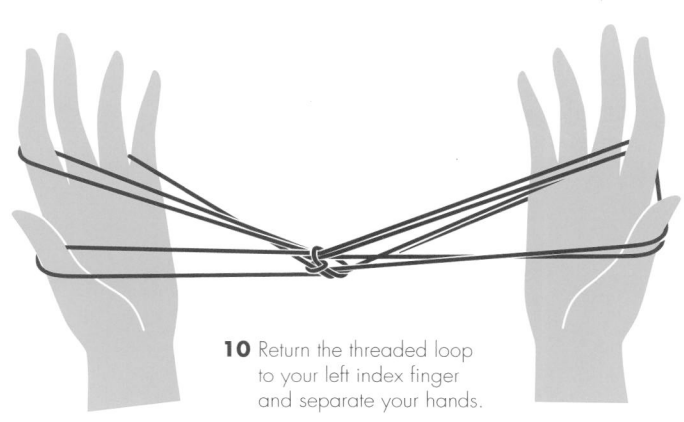

10 Return the threaded loop to your left index finger and separate your hands.

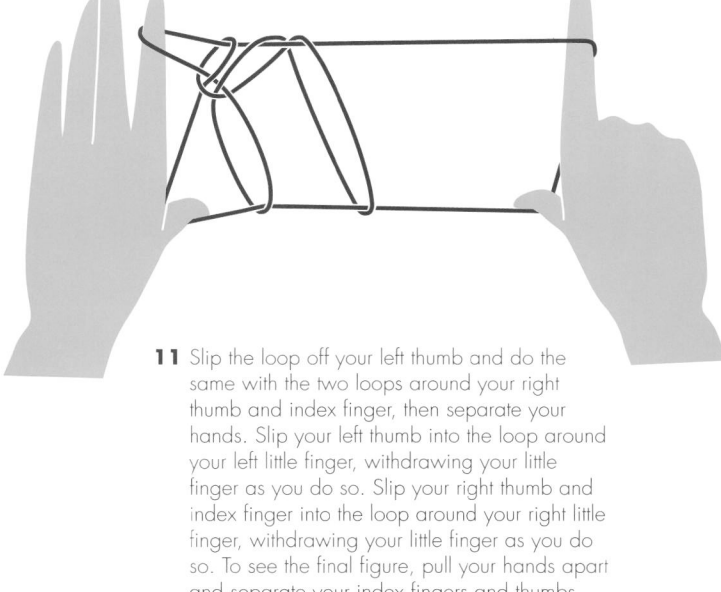

11 Slip the loop off your left thumb and do the same with the two loops around your right thumb and index finger, then separate your hands. Slip your left thumb into the loop around your left little finger, withdrawing your little finger as you do so. Slip your right thumb and index finger into the loop around your right little finger, withdrawing your little finger as you do so. To see the final figure, pull your hands apart and separate your index fingers and thumbs, pushing the thumbs slightly away from you.

Hard Cradles

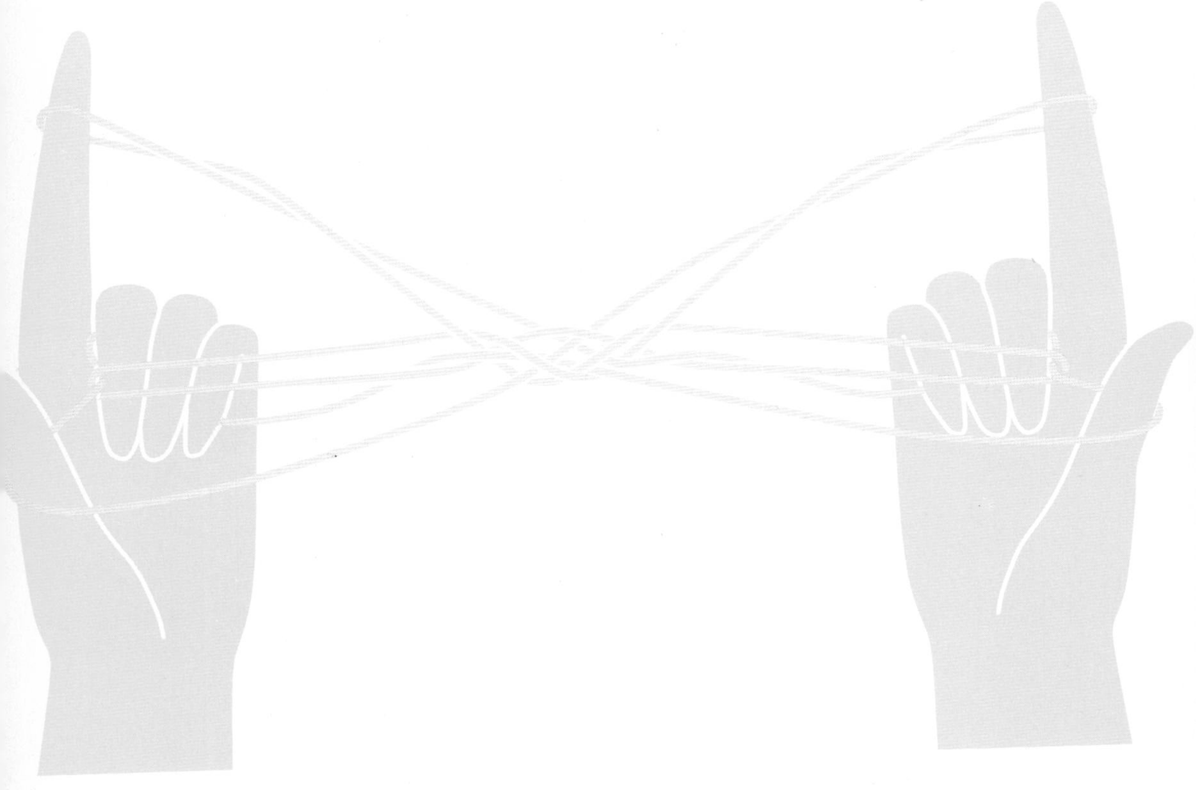

Now for the difficult ones. Leash the Dogs, at the start of the chapter, may lull you into a false sense of security, but don't be fooled – as you move on to the Rabbit and the Owl's Net you'll find that you need all your reserves of patience to master them. And the Coral Reef, the final figure in the book, is truly fiendish – you not only need to get all the moves right but you must also maintain the right amount of tension in the strings to achieve the final 'picture'. Get a friend to help you with the trickier moves (and ask them to adjust the tension manually, too, if you're having problems). And remember, you can always go back to some of the simple cradles if you need to relax before taking your skills further. Good luck, and good cradling.

Leashing the Dogs

This string sequence is found in a number of cultures and under
a wide variety of names. In the British Isles it's also known as
Leashing Lochiel's Dogs, although who Lochiel was and why
he had such a number of dogs does not survive in string lore.
Jayne credits the steps of the game to the Reverend John Gray,
who published them along with some other cat's cradles native
to Scotland in 1903, but the same figure had also been collected
in America, where the Cherokees named it Crow's Feet. It's a
complex and fiddly figure to carry through – particularly in Steps
10 and 11 – but the end result is satisfyingly neat.

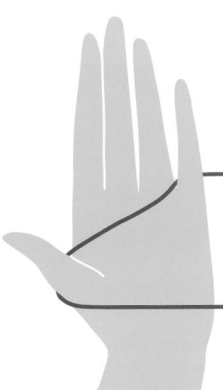
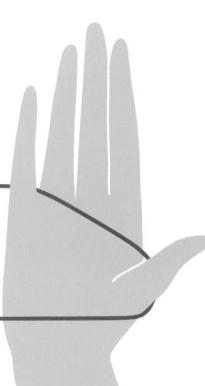

1 Loop the string across both palms and behind the little fingers and thumbs of both hands.

2 Place the index finger of your right hand under the palm string of your left and pull your hands apart.

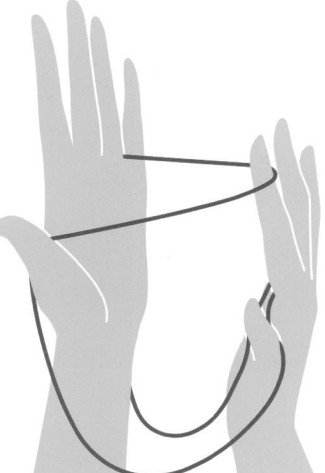

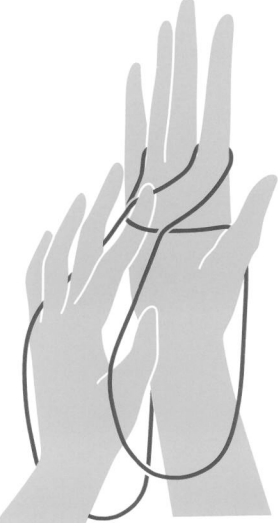

3 Repeat on the other side, placing the index finger of your left hand under the palm string of your right.

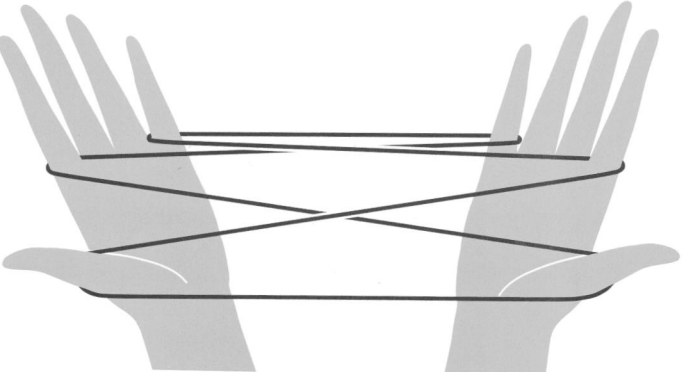

4 Pull your hands apart –
you'll have loops of string
around your little fingers,
index fingers and thumbs.

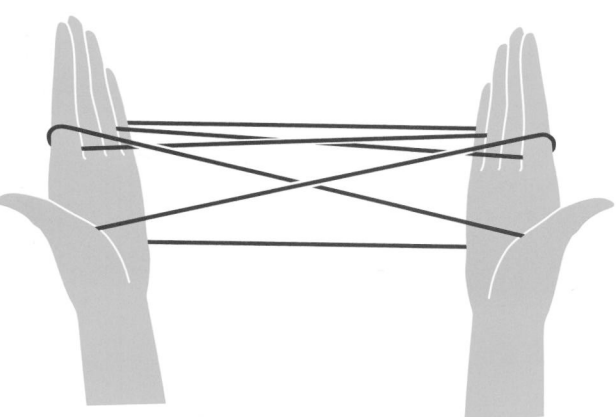

5 Turn your palms to face you, holding the
strings taut, and close all your fingers over
all the strings except for the string nearest
you, the one around your thumbs (shown
here on the left hand). Now turn your
hands first downwards and then back
up towards you, under the thumb string
(shown here on the right hand).

6 When your hands are
returned to their original
position the outer thumb
string will be around all
the fingers of both hands.

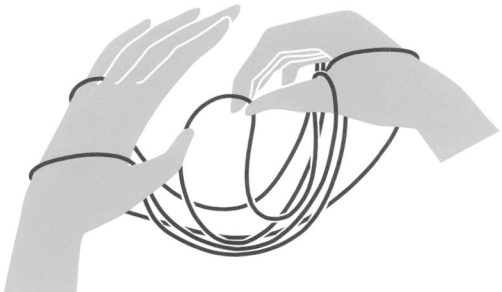

7 Use the thumb and index finger of your left hand to move the loop on your right index finger to your right thumb. Repeat on your left hand, using the thumb and index finger of your right hand to move the loop on your left index finger to your left thumb.

8 Use the thumb and index finger of your right hand to move the string across the back of your left hand on to just the middle finger. Repeat on the right hand, using the thumb and index finger of your left hand to move the string across the back of your right on to just your right middle finger.

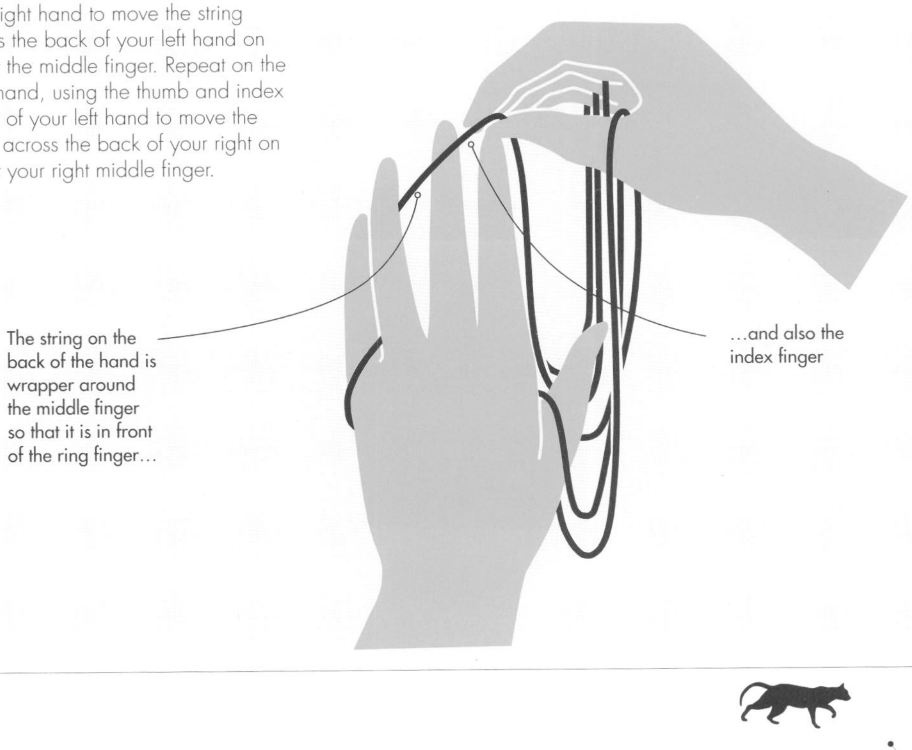

The string on the back of the hand is wrapper around the middle finger so that it is in front of the ring finger…

…and also the index finger

9 Pull your hands apart and, turning them slightly towards you, bend your little fingers over the middle-finger string furthest away from you and, bending them back and under, pick up the near little-finger string on their backs and bring them back upright to their original position.

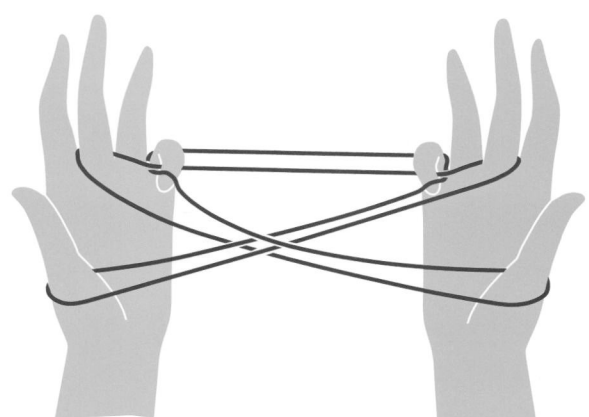

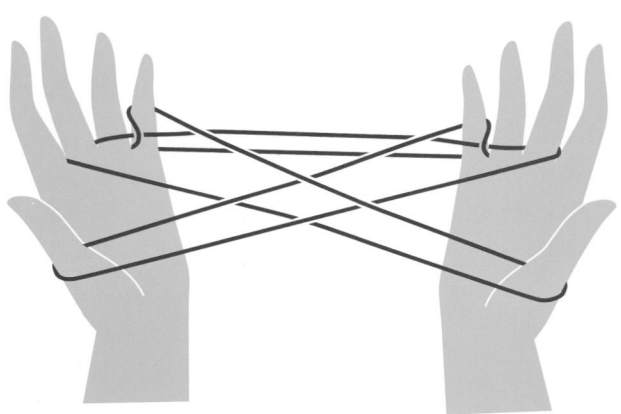

10 You should now have loops on the thumb and middle finger of each hand, while the two strings furthest away, around your little fingers, form loops around the further middle-finger string between your little and ring fingers.

11 Using the thumb and index finger of your right hand, pick up the string that runs across to your right little finger from your left little finger on the far side and take it over the tip of your left little finger.

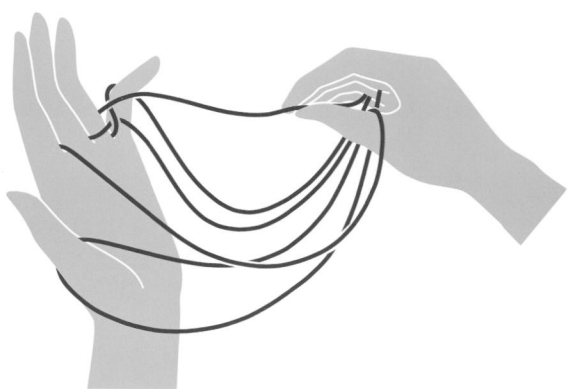

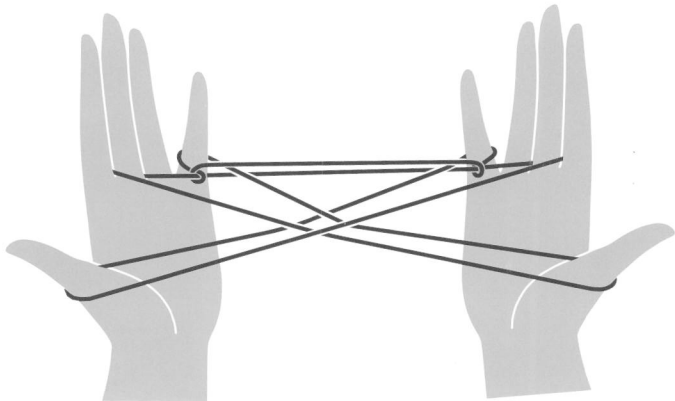

12 Repeat Step 11 on your right hand, using the thumb and index finger of your left to pick up the string that runs across to your left little finger from your right and take it over the tip of the little finger of your right hand. Pull your hands apart to tighten the strings.

13 Gently slip the loops from your thumbs and pull your hands apart. The fans of strings from the fingers of each hand are the dogs, while the two straight strings linking them make up the leash.

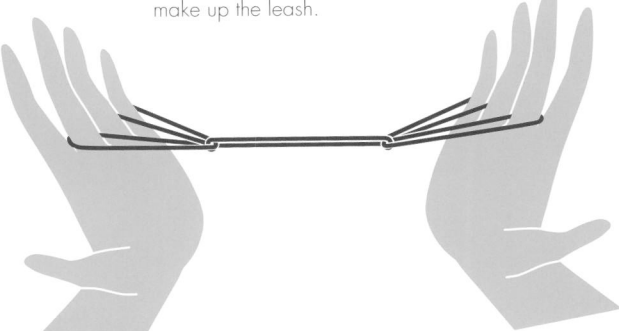

Caroline Islands Catch

Like so many other string figures, the Caroline Islands Catch was first collected in the islands of the Pacific by William Furness, brother of Caroline Furness Jayne, and she credits it to him in her popular collection of cat's cradles. It's the first of two net-shaped figures that feature in this chapter (the other is the Owl's Net – but don't try that until you can successfully complete this rather easier form). The 'catch' after which it's named comes right at the end; enlist another player for the final step.

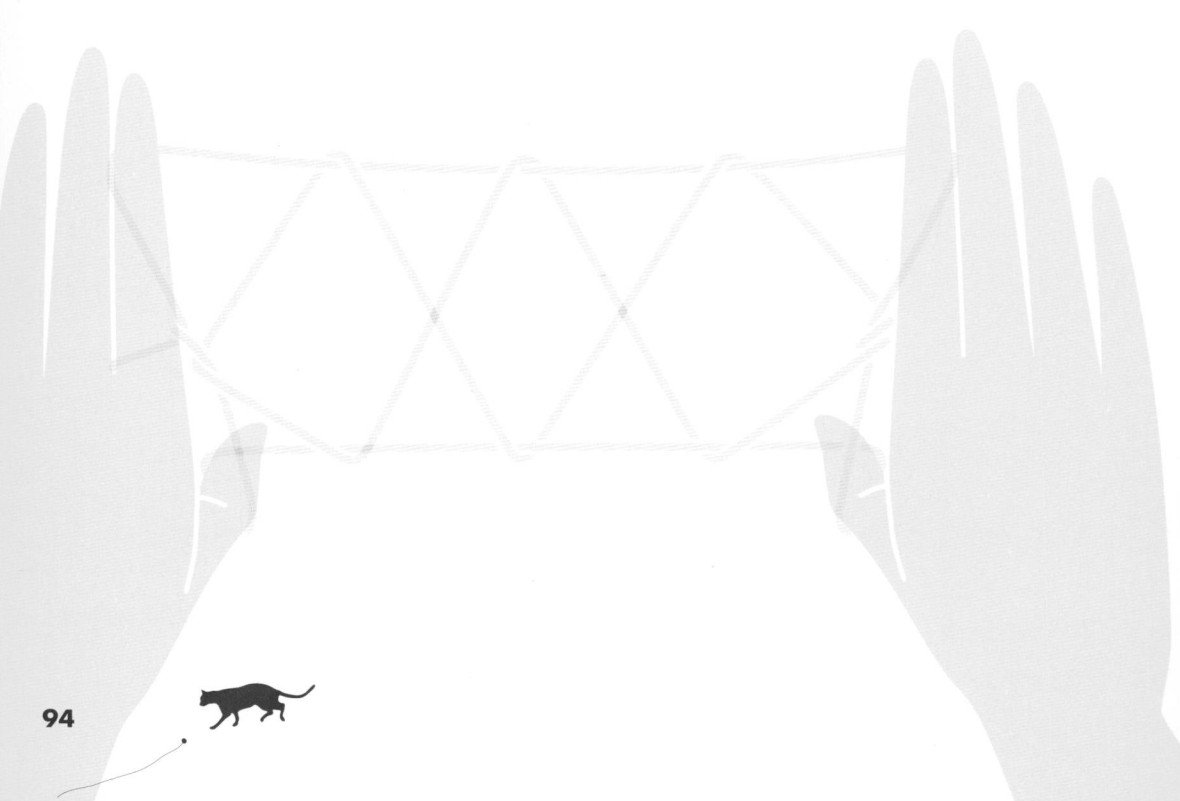

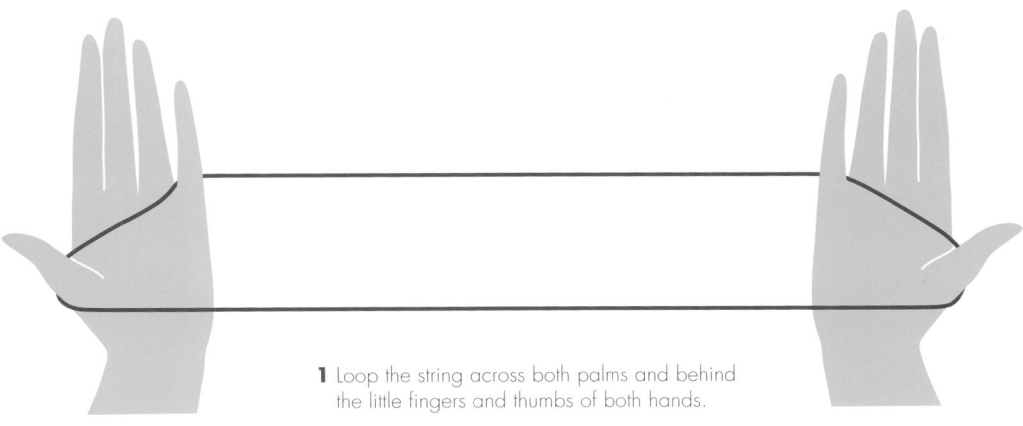

1 Loop the string across both palms and behind the little fingers and thumbs of both hands.

2 Place the index finger of your left hand under the palm string of your right and pull your hands apart.

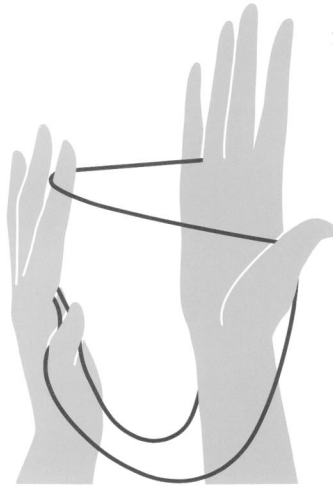

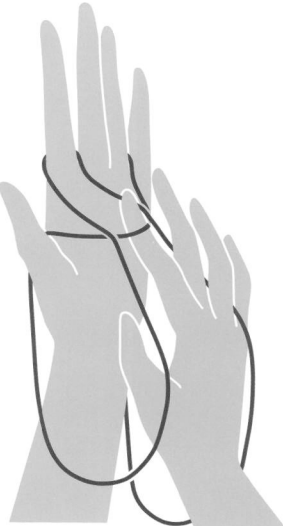

3 Repeat on the other side, placing the index finger of your right hand under the palm string of your left.

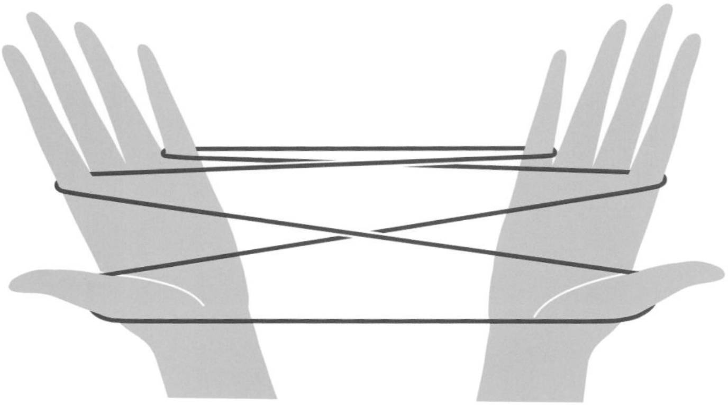

4 Pull your hands apart –
you'll have loops of string
around your little fingers,
index fingers and thumbs.

5 Gently slip your left hand out of
all the loops and hold your right
hand palm down, fingers facing left,
so that the loops are hanging down
from the palm. Put the tips of your
left thumb and little finger together
and pass them through the loop
hanging from your right index finger.

6 Once through the loop, pull your left thumb and
little finger apart, slip the loop off your right index
finger and separate your hands. The left hand is
now in the original first position but the right has
twisted loops around the thumb and little finger,
as well as a string across the palm.

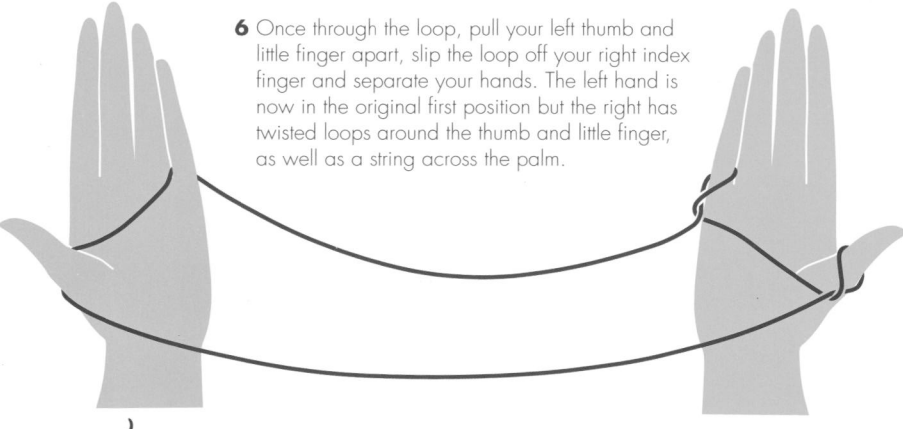

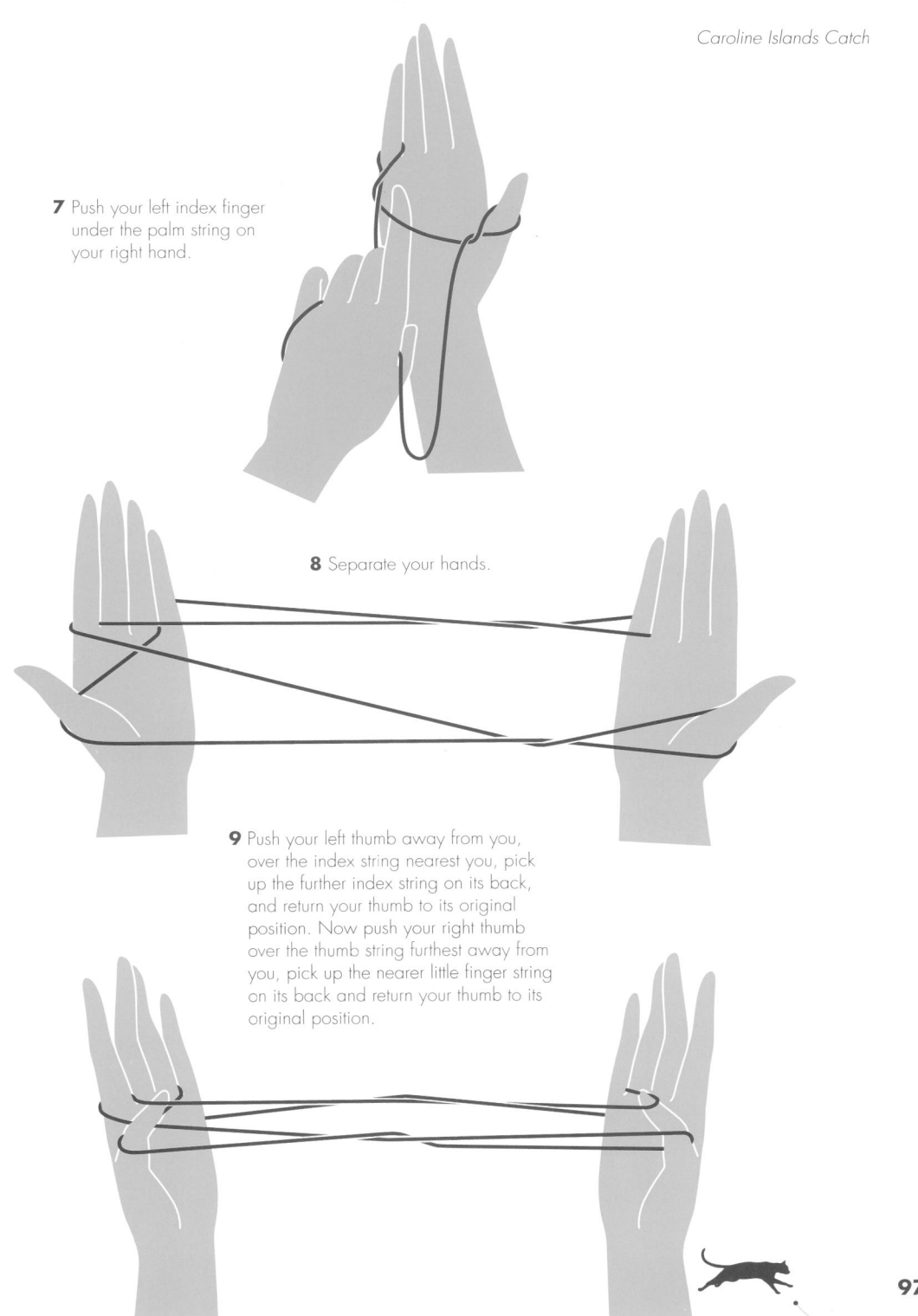

7 Push your left index finger under the palm string on your right hand.

8 Separate your hands.

9 Push your left thumb away from you, over the index string nearest you, pick up the further index string on its back, and return your thumb to its original position. Now push your right thumb over the thumb string furthest away from you, pick up the nearer little finger string on its back and return your thumb to its original position.

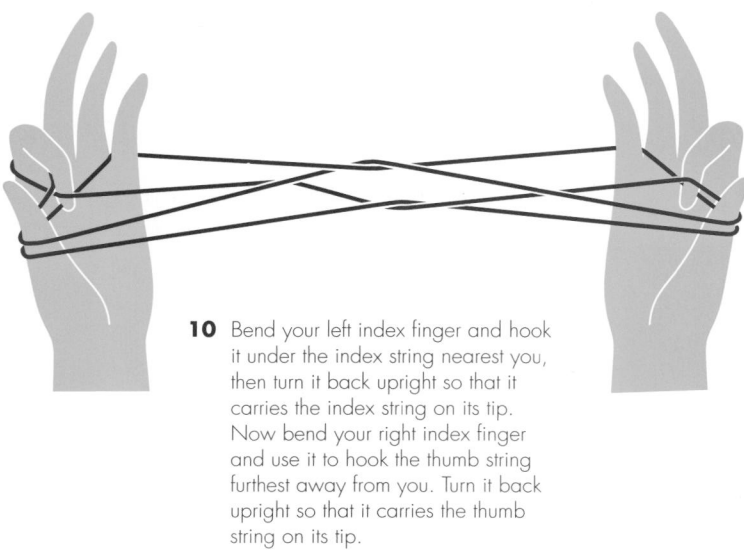

10 Bend your left index finger and hook it under the index string nearest you, then turn it back upright so that it carries the index string on its tip. Now bend your right index finger and use it to hook the thumb string furthest away from you. Turn it back upright so that it carries the thumb string on its tip.

11 Keep the strings on your index fingers near the tips by pressing your thumbs close to your index fingers, and hold both index fingers and thumbs very upright. Bend your little fingers over the far little-finger strings and use the little, ring and middle fingers of both hands to hold the little finger strings down on your palms.

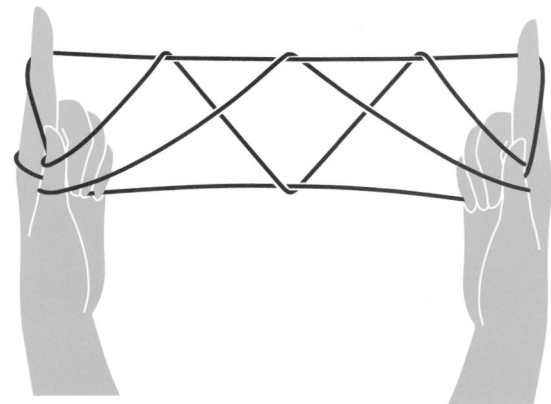

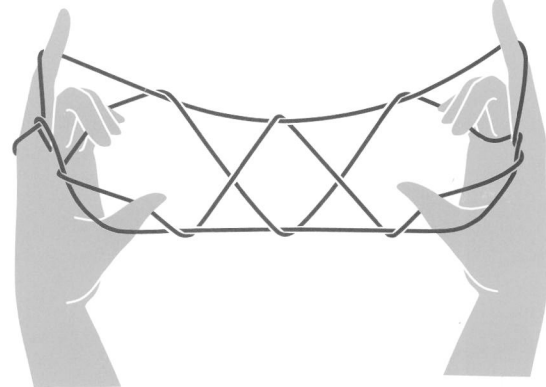

12 Use your teeth (you won't have fingers to spare!) to pull the lower loop on your left thumb up over the upper thumb loop and over the thumb tip so that it falls on the palm side. Repeat on the lower loop on your right thumb. The upper loops on both thumbs should remain in place.

13 Slip the loops off your little fingers and pull the figure taut between your thumbs and index fingers, turning your palms away from you and pointing your thumbs away, too.

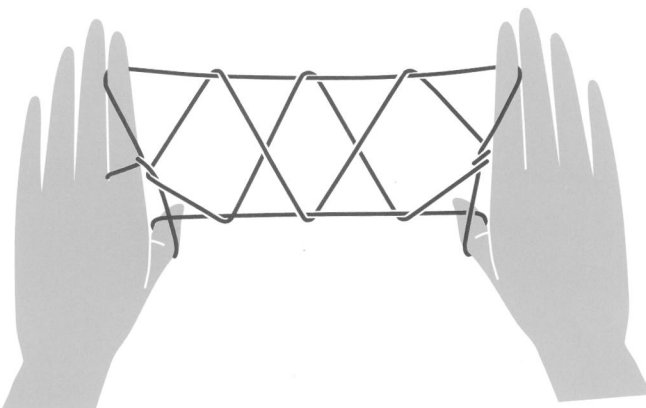

What's the catch? When the final figure is arranged, ask a friend to push their hand through the central diamond, then you can choose whether to free the hand or not – if you drop all the strings from your left hand and pull to the right, their hand will be caught in a tight loop; if, on the other hand, you drop all the strings from your right hand and pull to the left, their hand will instantly be freed as the string falls away.

The Well

This is probably the easiest of a number of quite similar figures collected in the Pacific. It features in a collection published in 1906 called *Cat's Cradles from Many Lands* by Kathleen Haddon, who gave it a provenance in the Loyalty Islands, part of New Caledonia. A similar figure from the Torres Straits is called the Nest and a rare string figure from Northern India called the Fishing Boat shares several of the later steps. The maker can make the end shape deeper or shallower – 'filling' or 'emptying' the well – by changing the angle of their thumbs in the last couple of steps.

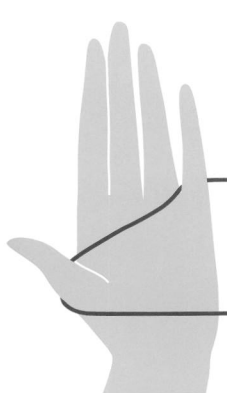
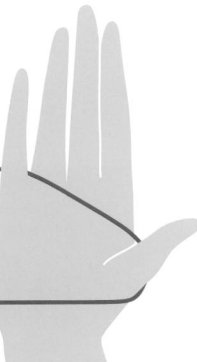

1 Loop the string across both palms and behind the little fingers and thumbs of both hands.

2 Place the index finger of your right hand under the palm string of your left and pull your hands apart.

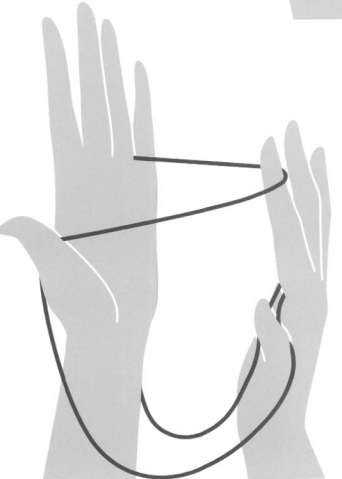

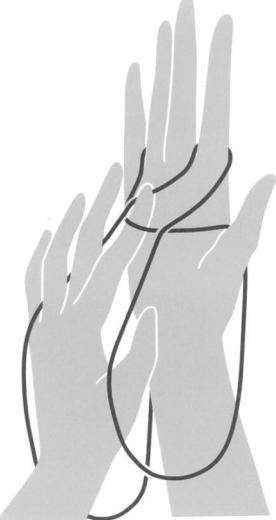

3 Repeat on the other side, placing the index finger of your left hand under the palm string of your right.

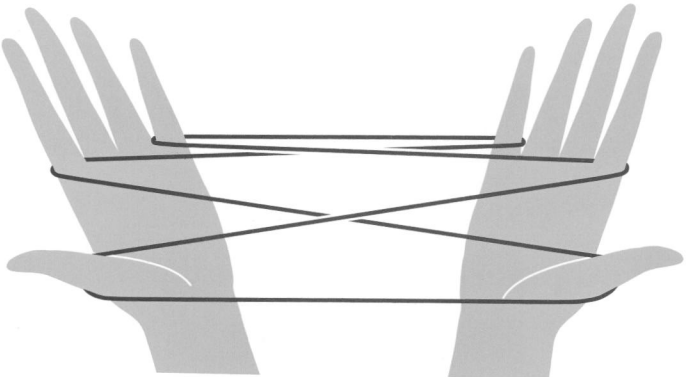

4 Pull your hands apart –
you'll have loops of string
around your little fingers,
index fingers and thumbs.

5 Take your index fingers over the far index string and push
them into the loops around the little fingers. Turning your
palms slightly towards you, bend your index fingers and
bring them back towards you (you'll be carrying two
strings on each), bringing them up between the near
index strings and your thumbs. As you do so, the near
index string will slip off your index fingers.

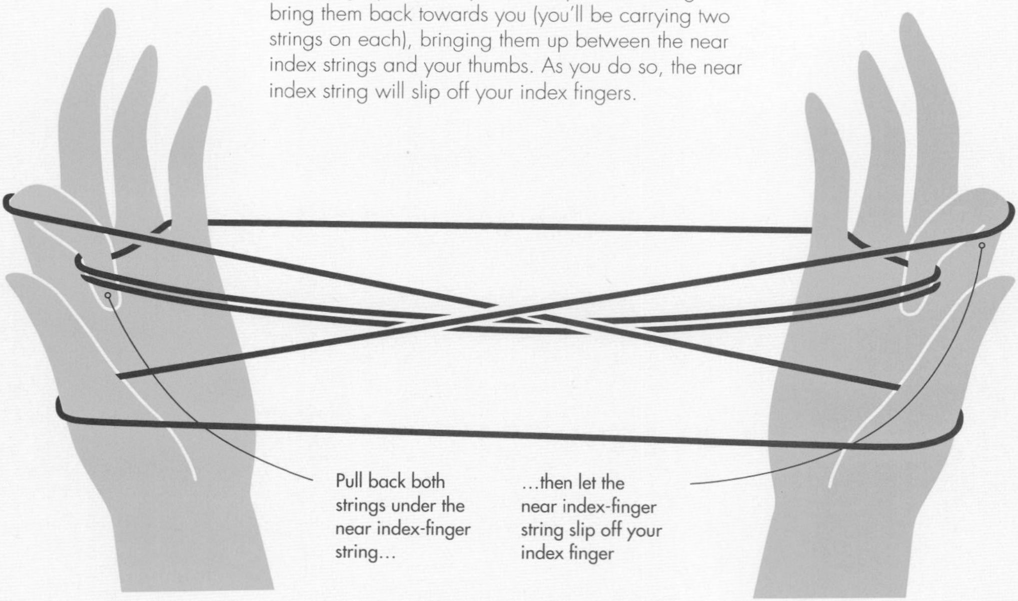

Pull back both
strings under the
near index-finger
string…

…then let the
near index-finger
string slip off your
index finger

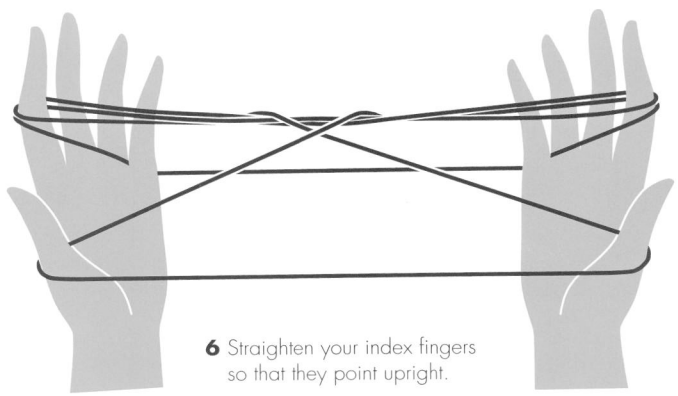

6 Straighten your index fingers so that they point upright.

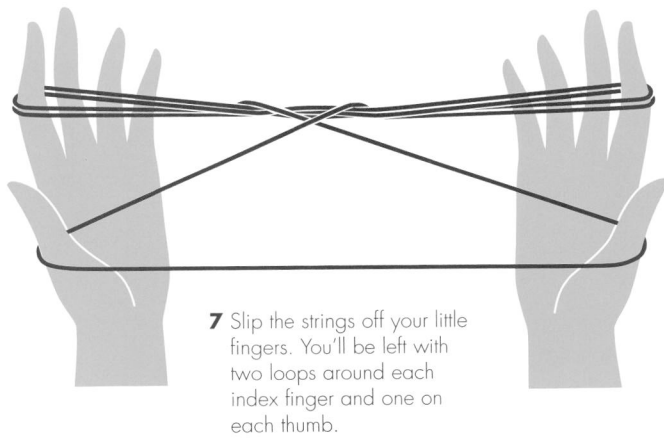

7 Slip the strings off your little fingers. You'll be left with two loops around each index finger and one on each thumb.

8 Holding the middle, ring and little fingers of each hand together, use them to push down on the two strings on your index fingers furthest away from you.

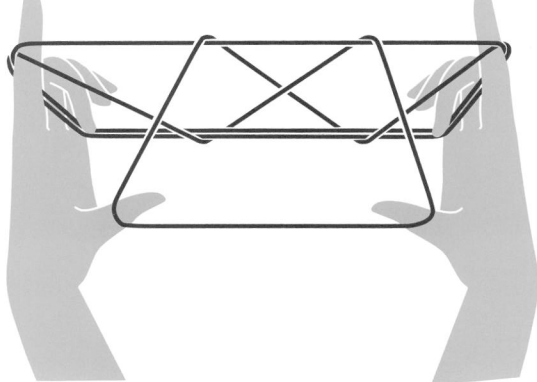

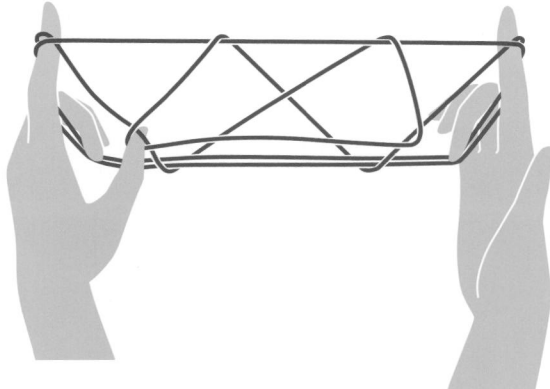

9 Gently slip your thumbs out from their loops while holding the string figure loosely, without pulling (because the second part of this step is the hardest part of the figure). The released loops will hang from the straight top string of the figure. Bend your thumbs back through these loops, pick up the diagonal string that leads from the index to the bottom of the figure on the back of your thumbs (shown here on the left hand) and pull it back towards you through the hanging loop.

10 Straighten your thumbs back towards you and turn your index fingers slightly away from you while continuing to hold the lowest two strings of the figure down with your middle, ring and little fingers held together. The final shape of the well will emerge.

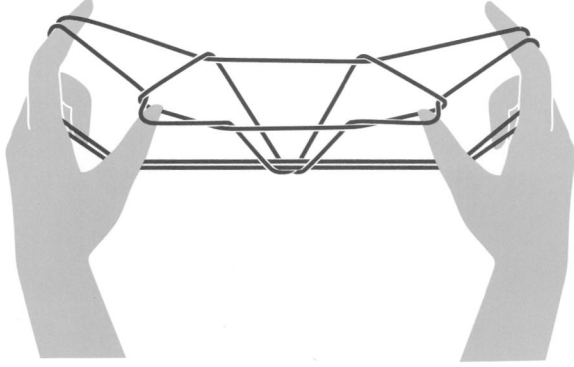

The Rabbit

While it requires a good imagination to see the advertised shape in some of the classic old-style string figures, if you can work your way through to the end of this one it offers a refreshingly clear picture of the bunny's face and big ears with the final move. It's one of the harder exercises in this book: after a simple beginning the moves become increasingly fiddly and the twelfth and final step is likely to need a little experimentation. If the rabbit doesn't appear distinctly, shift the relative positions of your fingers and hands around slightly – chances are that the tensions between the strings aren't balanced quite right and so are pulling the figure out of shape.

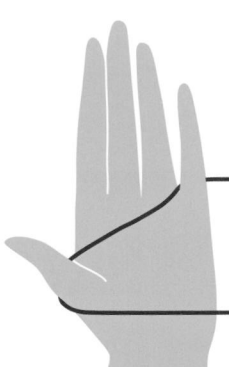
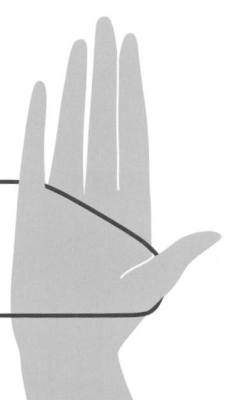

1 Loop the string across both palms and behind the little fingers and thumbs of both hands.

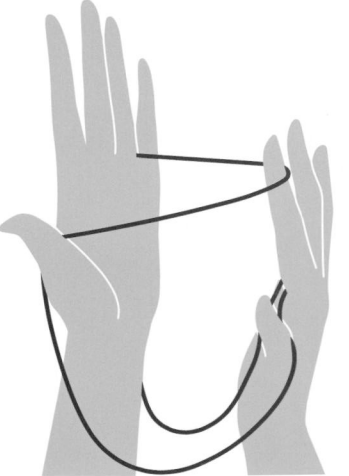

2 Place the index finger of your right hand under the palm string of your left and pull your hands apart.

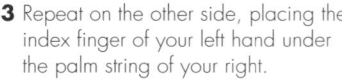
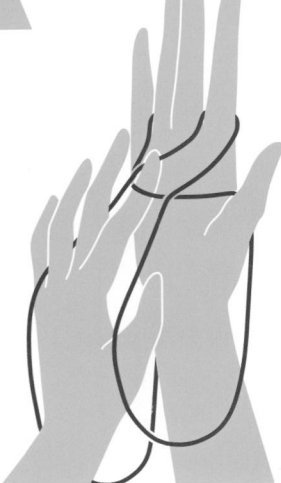

3 Repeat on the other side, placing the index finger of your left hand under the palm string of your right.

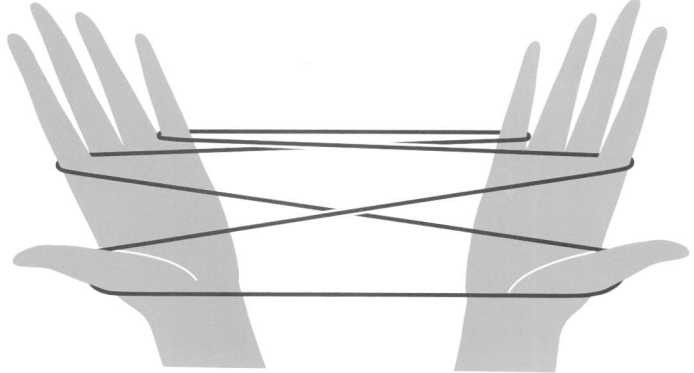

4 Pull your hands apart –
you'll have loops of string
around your little fingers,
index fingers and thumbs.

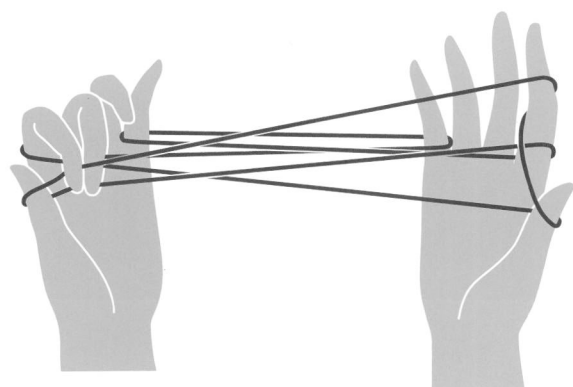

5 Bend your middle fingers into the loops
around your thumbs and your index fingers
down on the outside of the thumb strings
nearest to you, and, using these paired
fingers to hold the outer thumb string
(shown here on the left hand), turn your
palms slightly away from you and slip this
string on to the tips of your index fingers
(shown here on the right hand).

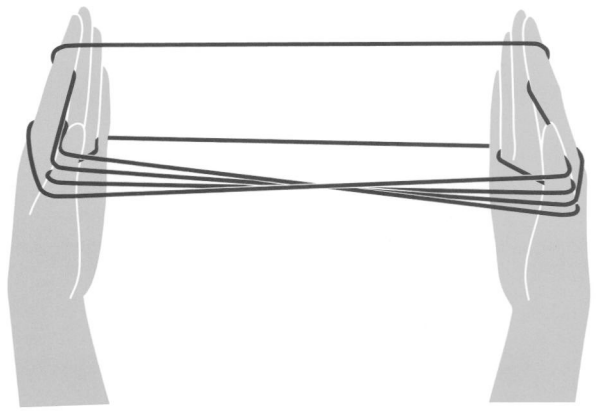

6 Slip the loops off your thumbs, keeping all the other strings taut. Push your thumbs into the loop around your little finger from below and then pull them back towards you. They will be carrying four strings with them (the near little finger string, the upper far index string and both strings of the lower loop on the index fingers).

7 Push your thumbs up and over the upper string around your index fingers and nearest to you, and pull this string down with the tops of your thumbs, letting the other loops slip off your thumbs as you do. This move calls for a little more dexterity than usual – it's hard to keep your thumbs hooked over the top string to hold it in place while slipping the other strings off them. If all the strings slip off, take a deep breath, count to ten and go back to the beginning of the figure.

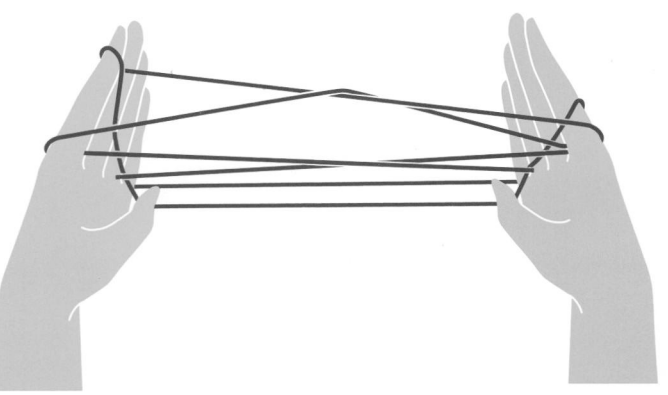

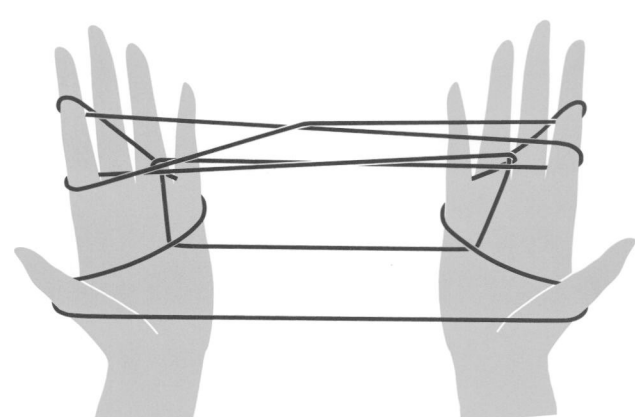

8 While still retaining the string on your upper thumbs, push them away from you under the little-finger string furthest from you and pull it back towards you on the backs of your thumbs (the original string will slip from the thumbs with this backwards movement).

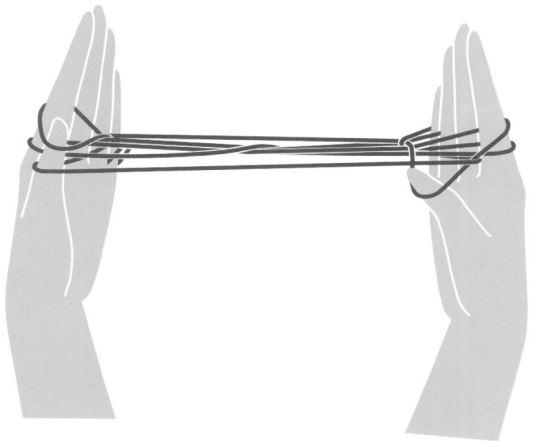

9 Push your thumbs upwards into the upper loops around the index fingers (shown here on the left hand) and pull the near strings of these loops downwards through the loops around the thumbs, slipping the original loops off the thumbs as you do so (shown here on the right hand).

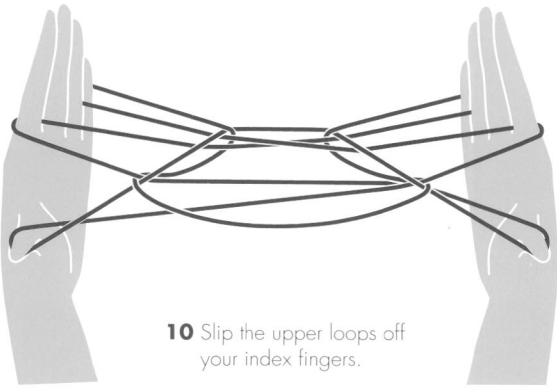

10 Slip the upper loops off your index fingers.

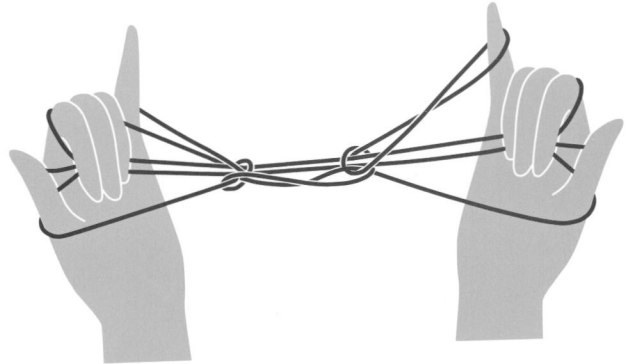

11 Holding the index, middle and ring fingers of both hands together, push them down into the loops around your thumbs, then slip the loops off your little fingers and push them into the thumb loops, too.

12 Hold all four fingers of both hands down on your palms and turn your hands so that your palms face you as you do so. Use the tips of your index fingers to lift up the thumb strings nearest you, slipping your thumbs out. In the final figure, your middle, ring and little fingers will be folded down, your index fingers and thumbs will be pointing upwards. If all the moves are correct but you can't see the rabbit, enlist a friend to move some strings manually. When the rabbit does make an appearance, you may wish to take a photograph for posterity!

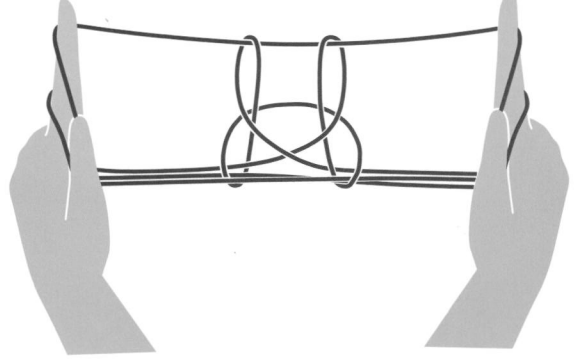

The Owl's Net

If you've already mastered Two-man Diamonds on pages 76–80 and the Caroline Islands Catch on pages 94–9, the Owl's Net naturally follows on as the most complicated of the three net patterns featured in this book. It is Native American in origin – Jayne records that it was collected in Virginia from a member of the Klamath tribe. The Owl's Net is straightforward enough to begin with but proves complex to finish correctly (from step 12 onwards), and calls for especially nimble fingers. Practise with a few simpler games before you try it out.

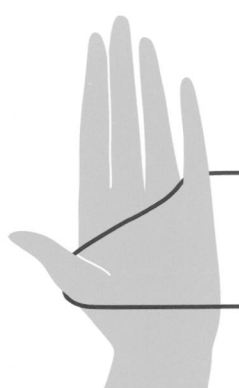
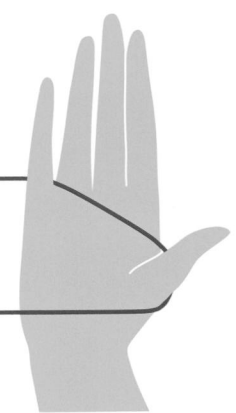

1 Loop the string across both palms and behind the little fingers and thumbs of both hands.

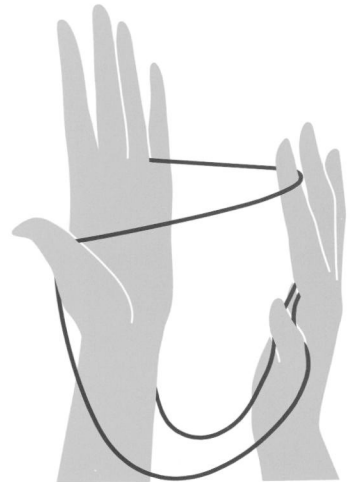

2 Place the index finger of your right hand under the palm string of your left and pull your hands apart.

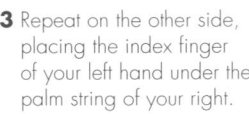

3 Repeat on the other side, placing the index finger of your left hand under the palm string of your right.

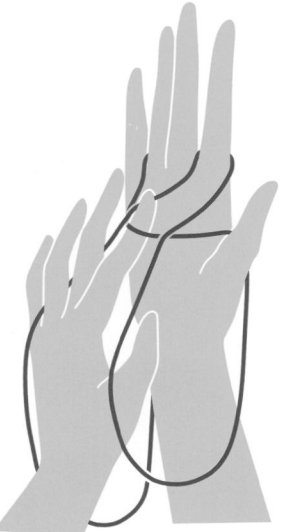

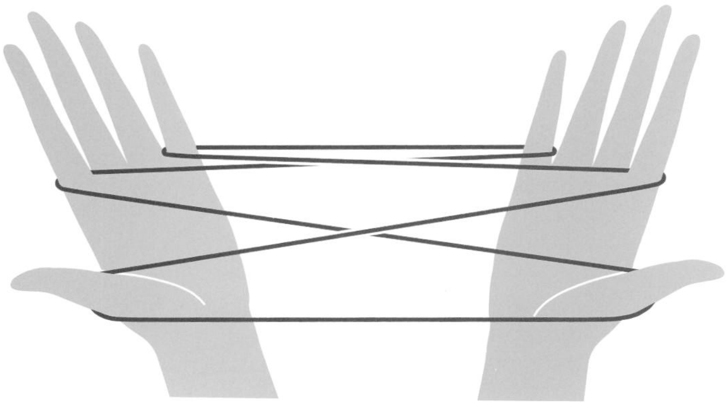

4 Pull your hands apart –
you'll have loops of string
around your little fingers,
index fingers and thumbs.

5 Turn your thumbs away from
you, taking them over the far
thumb strings and the index
finger strings nearest you and
under the further index strings.
Pick the further index strings up
from below, on the backs of your
thumbs, and bring your thumbs
back to their original position.

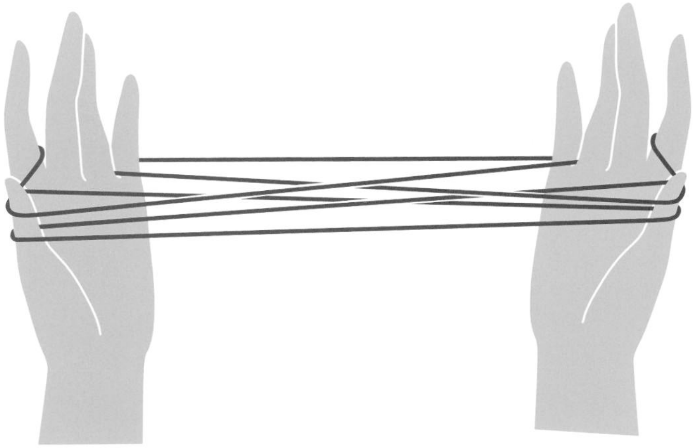

6 Push your index and middle fingers
down into the upper thumb loop,
then place your index fingers on
the side of the lower thumb string
nearest you and your middle
fingers into the lower thumb loop.
Clasp the lower thumb string
between your paired fingers.

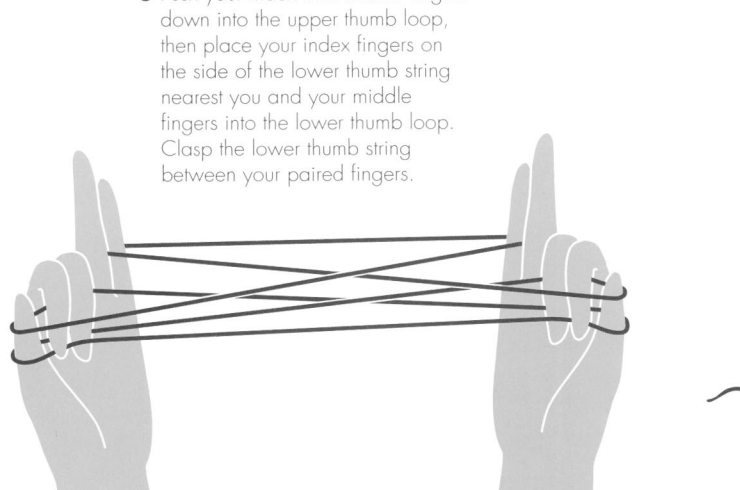

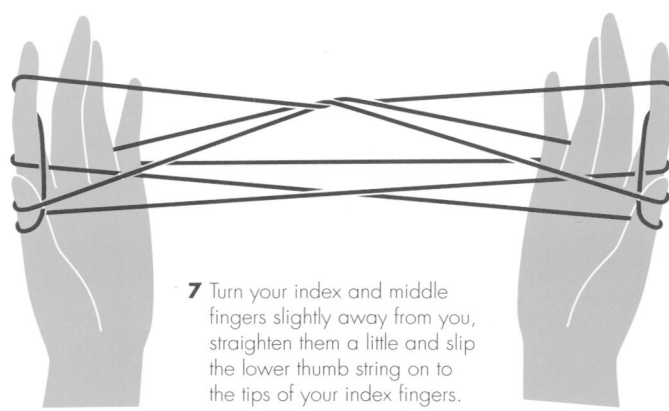

7 Turn your index and middle fingers slightly away from you, straighten them a little and slip the lower thumb string on to the tips of your index fingers.

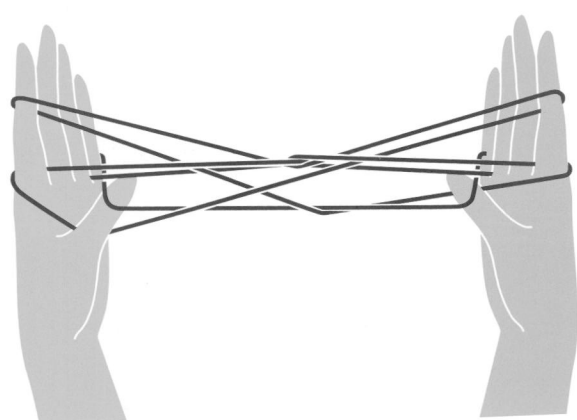

8 Release the loops around your thumbs, then push your thumbs away from you, taking them over the index-finger strings nearest you and under all the other strings. Pick up the outermost string (outside your little fingers) with the backs of your thumbs (shown here on the left hand) and bring your thumbs back to their original position, slipping the loops off your little fingers as you do so (shown here on the right hand).

9 Turning your palms slightly towards you, put the little, ring and middle fingers of both hands into the loops around your thumbs. Close the fingers across your palms to hold the strings down, slipping your thumbs out of the loops as you do so. Push your freed thumbs upwards into the upper loops on your index fingers, and slip your index fingers out of them, so the loops are transferred to your thumbs.

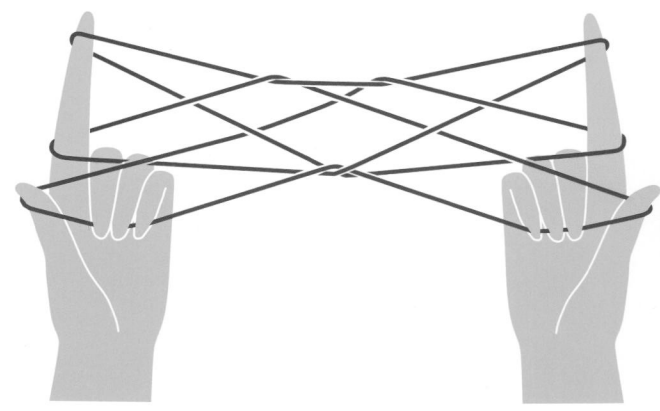

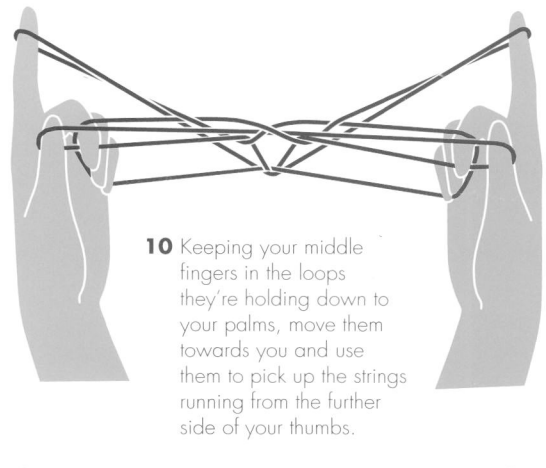

10 Keeping your middle fingers in the loops they're holding down to your palms, move them towards you and use them to pick up the strings running from the further side of your thumbs.

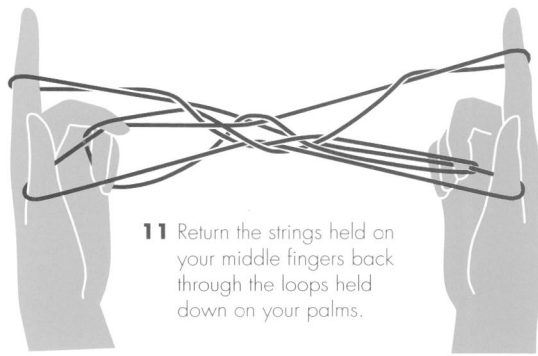

11 Return the strings held on your middle fingers back through the loops held down on your palms.

12 Slip your ring and little fingers out of the loops they're holding and push them towards you into the loops alongside your middle fingers.

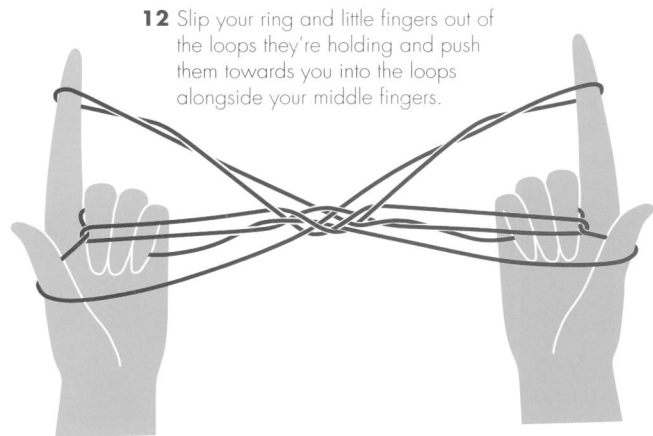

13 Push your middle fingers towards you, between the strings that form loops around the strings running across your palms, and bend each middle finger over the lower of these strings (shown here on the left hand) then draw these lower strings away from you, releasing the loops held by your ring and little fingers (shown here on the right hand).

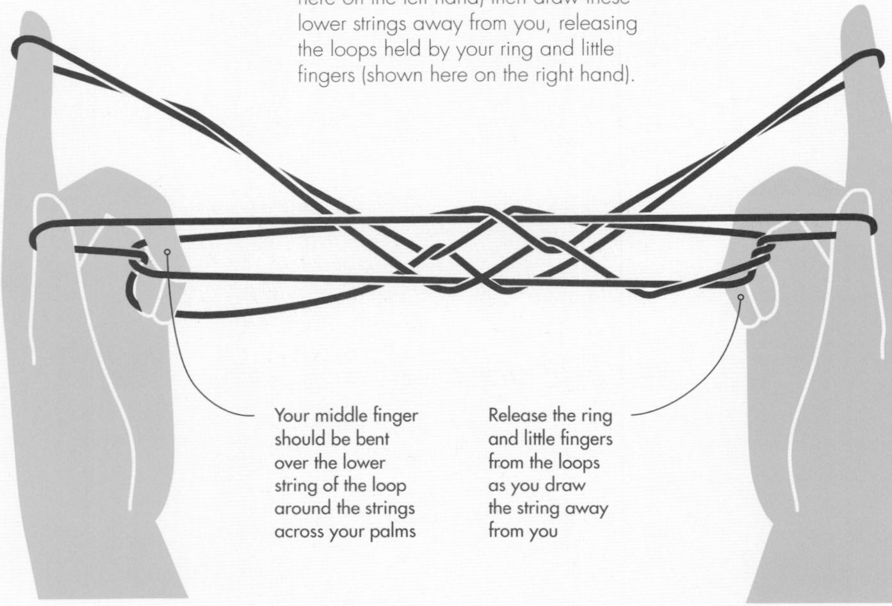

Your middle finger should be bent over the lower string of the loop around the strings across your palms

Release the ring and little fingers from the loops as you draw the string away from you

14 Now put your ring and little fingers into the loops held down by your middle fingers. At the same time, withdraw your middle fingers and hold them upright.

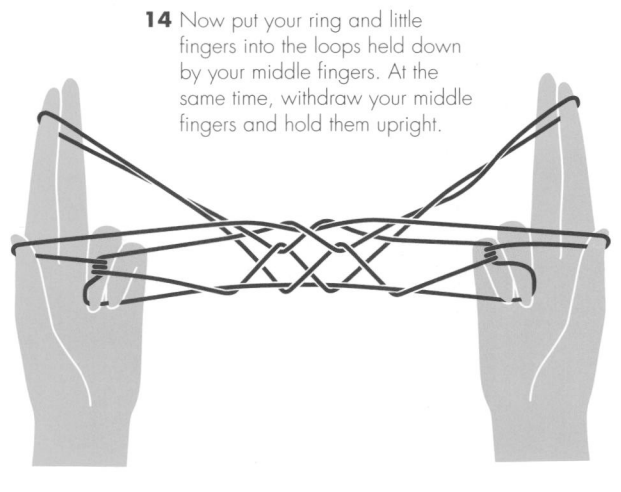

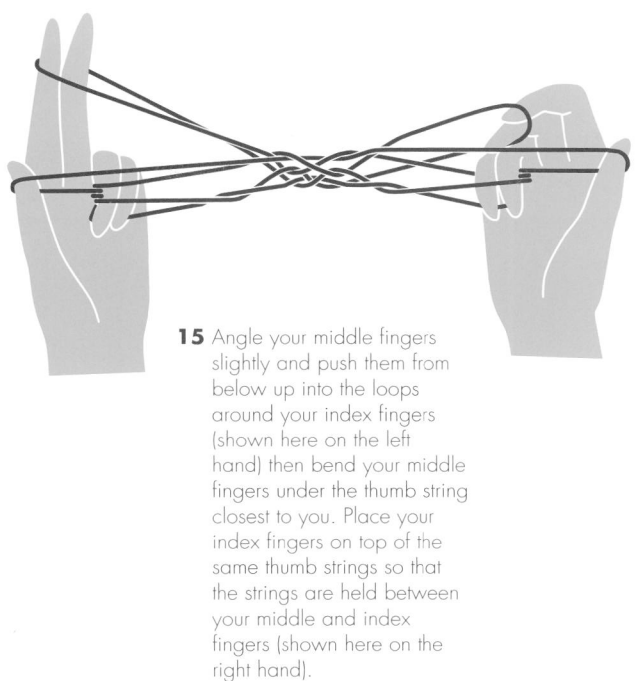

15 Angle your middle fingers
slightly and push them from
below up into the loops
around your index fingers
(shown here on the left
hand) then bend your middle
fingers under the thumb string
closest to you. Place your
index fingers on top of the
same thumb strings so that
the strings are held between
your middle and index
fingers (shown here on the
right hand).

16 Turn your index and middle fingers slightly away from
you, allowing the index loop to slip from the fingers.
Now turn your palms slightly outwards, at the same
time slipping the thumb strings on to the tips of your
index fingers. To form the final figure, slip the loops
off your thumbs and separate your hands.

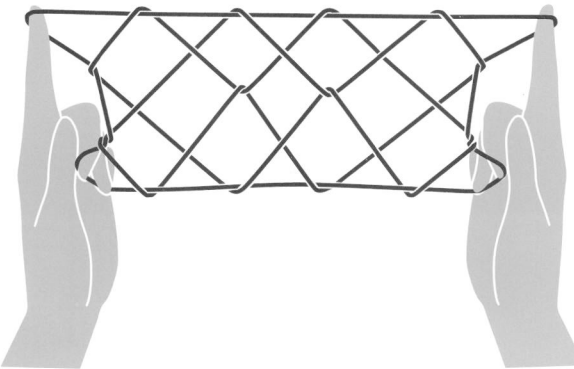

Coral Reef

Another figure from the Caroline Islands, this was first noted –
named simply Coral – by Dr William Furness, the anthropologist
brother of Caroline Furness Jayne. It's a notably difficult form – the
pièce de résistance of the string enthusiast – and if you can make
it successfully you can reasonably regard yourself as a cat's-cradle
expert. As usual when attempting the toughest string games,
practise each step several times as you work your way through
the sequence; if you try to push straight through to the end you're
unlikely to complete the figure. Be warned, though, it calls for both
an unusual degree of dexterity and plenty of patience.

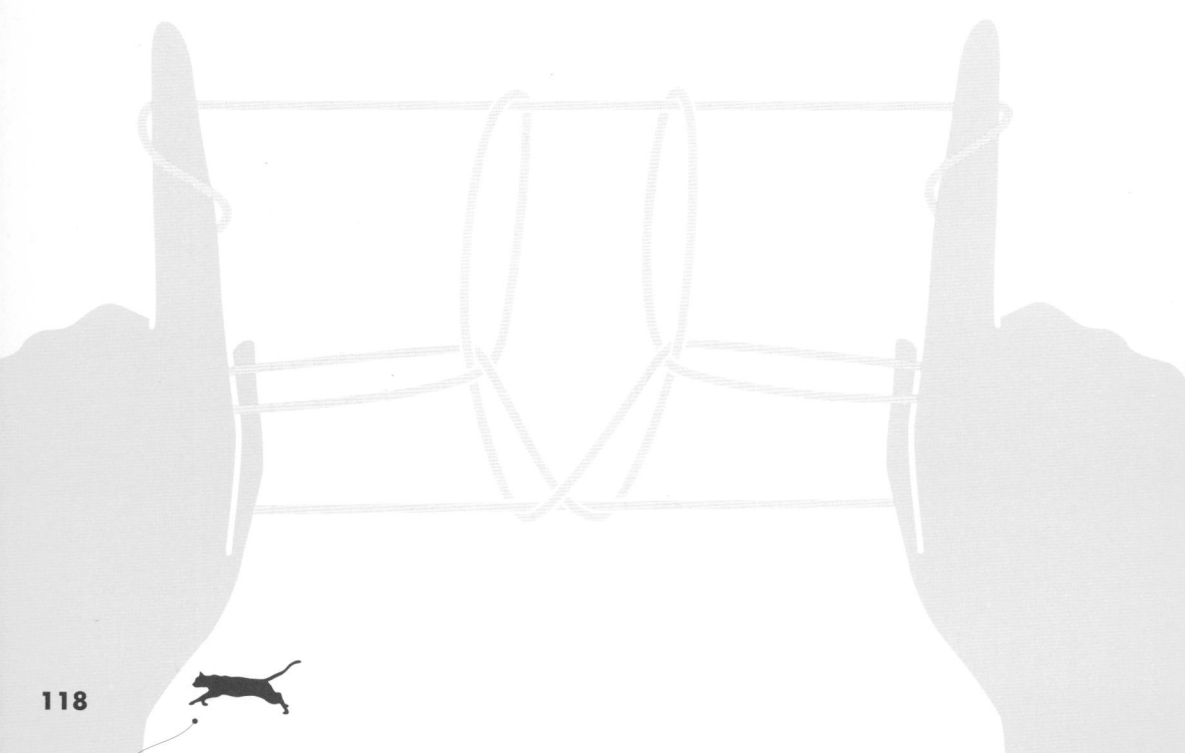

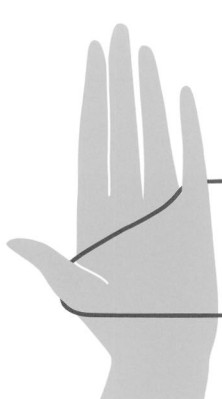 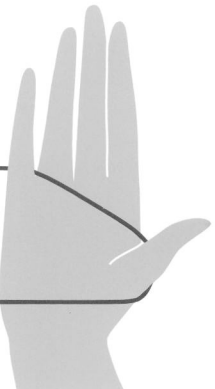

1 Loop the string across both palms and behind the little fingers and thumbs of both hands.

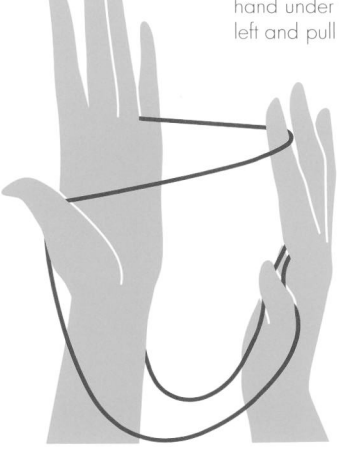

2 Place the index finger of your right hand under the palm string of your left and pull your hands apart.

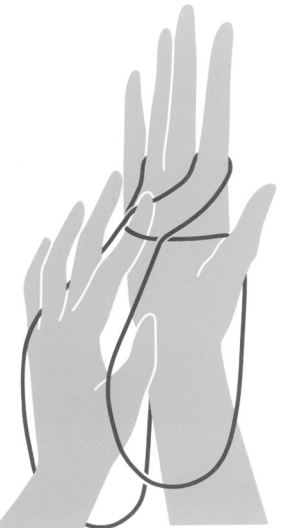

3 Repeat on the other side, placing the index finger of your left hand under the palm string of your right.

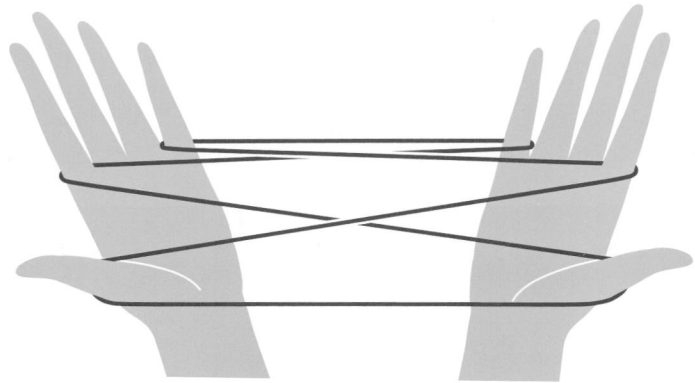

4 Pull your hands apart – you'll have loops of string around your little fingers, index fingers and thumbs.

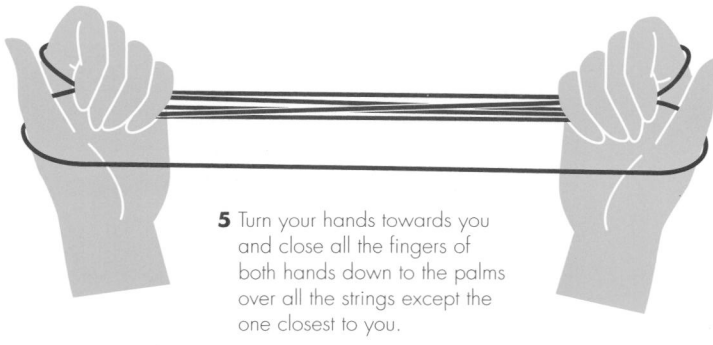

5 Turn your hands towards you and close all the fingers of both hands down to the palms over all the strings except the one closest to you.

6 Keeping hold of the strings under your fingers, turn your hands down and then up towards you. The turn of your hands will move the string that was around the thumb and place it across the backs of your hands.

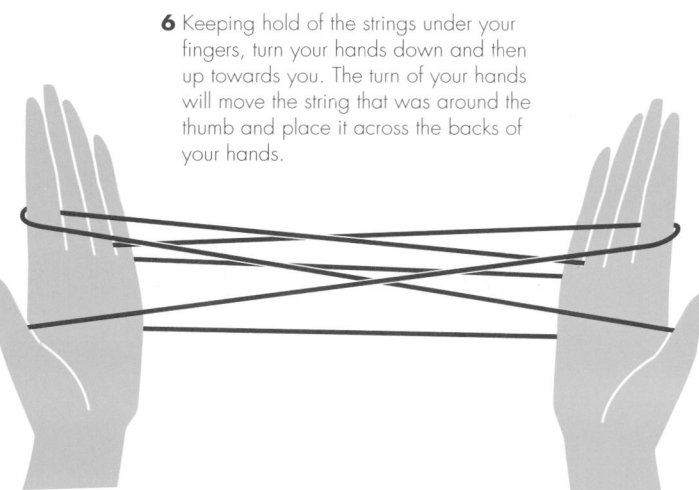

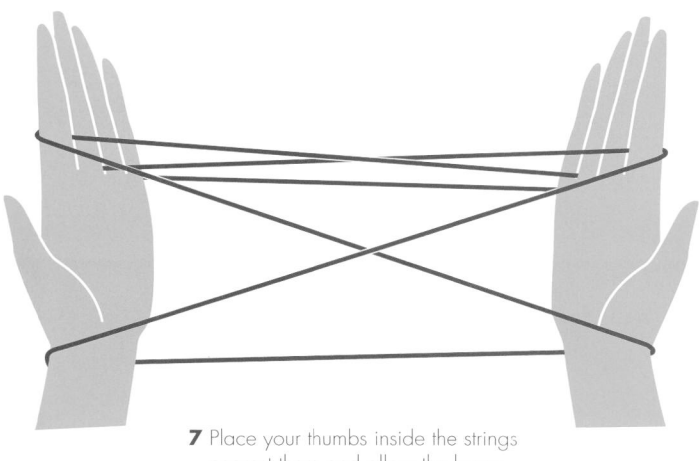

7 Place your thumbs inside the strings nearest them and allow the loops to slip down so that there is a loop around each wrist.

8 Turn your hands slightly towards you and pass your thumbs under both wrist strings. You'll find this easier to do if you hold the strings taut.

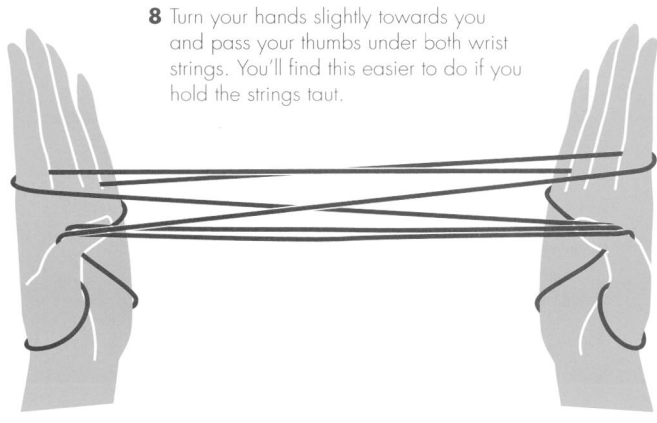

9 Push your thumbs from below up into the loops around your little fingers and use them to catch the little-finger strings furthest away from you.

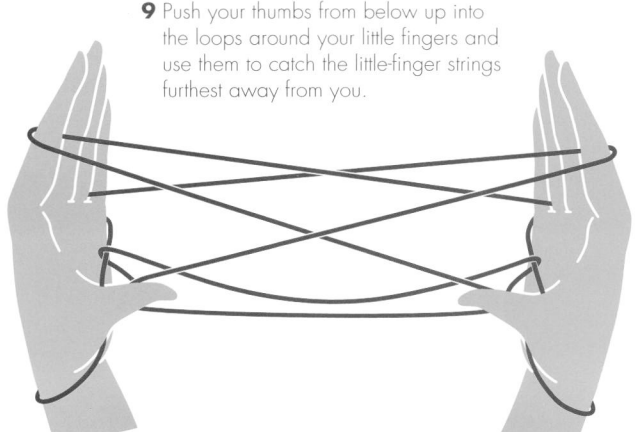

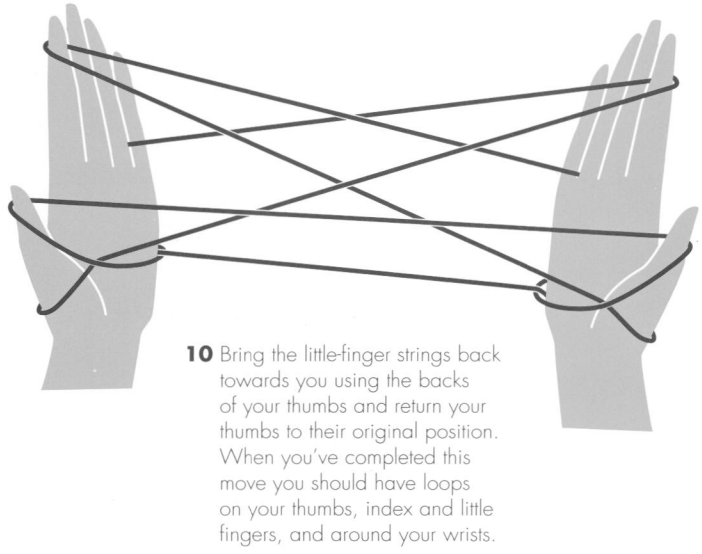

10 Bring the little-finger strings back towards you using the backs of your thumbs and return your thumbs to their original position. When you've completed this move you should have loops on your thumbs, index and little fingers, and around your wrists.

11 Use the thumb and index finger of your left hand to transfer the loop on your right thumb to your left thumb. Then use the thumb and index finger of your right hand to move the loop on your left thumb to your right thumb. Don't twist the strings as you move the loops.

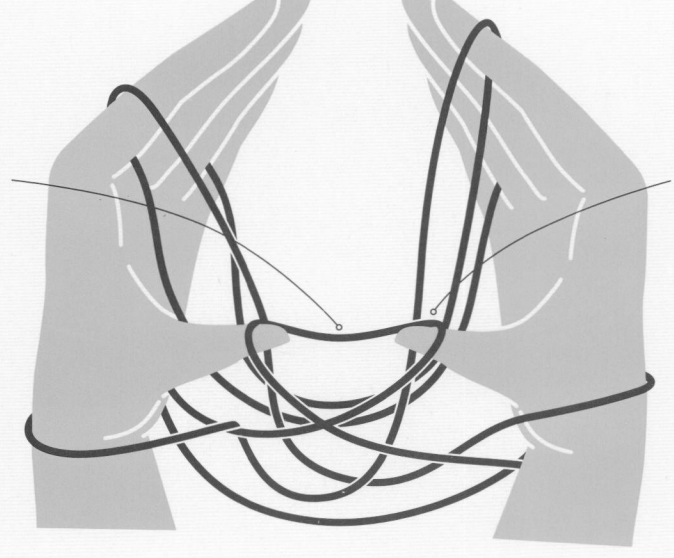

The loops around your thumbs are swapped over

Make sure don't twist these strings when you pass the loops from thumb to thumb

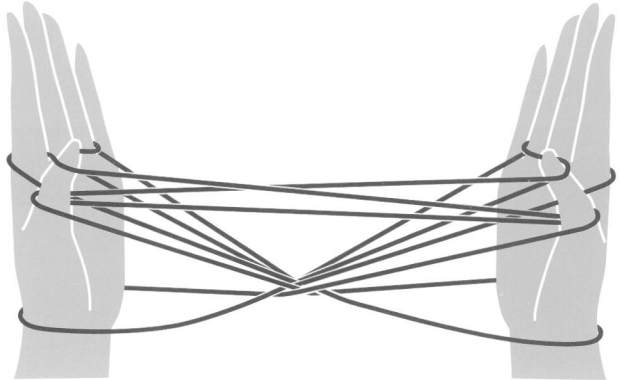

12 Move your thumbs away from you, taking them over the furthest thumb strings and both the strings around your index fingers, then pick up the nearest little-finger string with their backs and return your thumbs to their original positions, bringing the string with them.

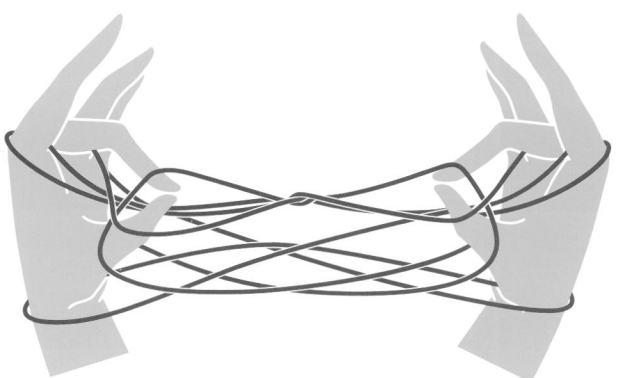

13 Bend your middle fingers down over the cross-palm strings and both the strings around the index fingers and use them to pick up the thumb strings furthest from you.

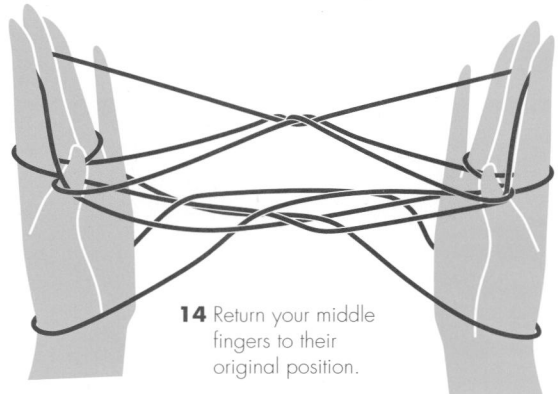

14 Return your middle
fingers to their
original position.

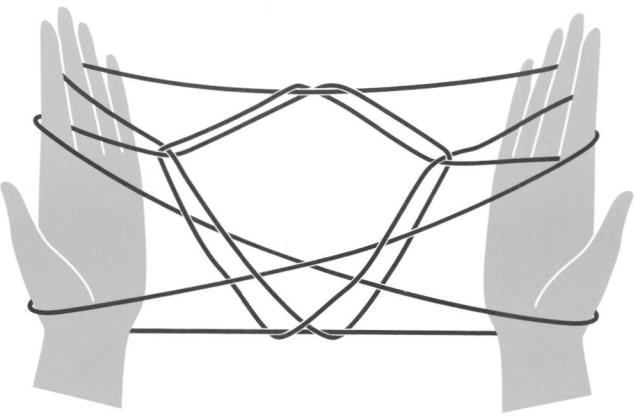

15 Slip the loops from your thumbs and little fingers
and separate your hands while keeping the strings
relaxed. If they are too taut at this stage you'll find
it harder to get through the next steps.

16 Turning your palms slightly towards you, use your left thumb and index finger to pick up the right wrist string from the nearer edge of the wrist.

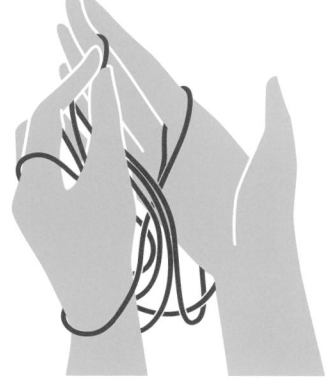

17 Pulling the wrist string out slightly, place it on the middle finger of your right hand.

18 Now for the really tricky stages – try to make the remaining moves smoothly and don't hold the strings too taut until you reach the final step of the figure.

Using your left thumb and index finger, pick up both strings from your right middle finger and carefully slip your right hand out of all the loops. Your left thumb and index finger should be left holding two loops, one longer and looping further to the right than the other.

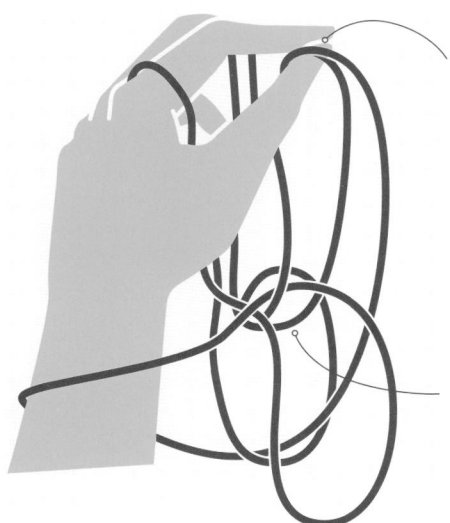

You should be holding the two loops from your right middle finger

The other loops from your right hand will be hanging loosely

19 Push the little finger of your right hand through the larger of the two loops held by the thumb and index finger of your left and push your right thumb away from you through both loops.

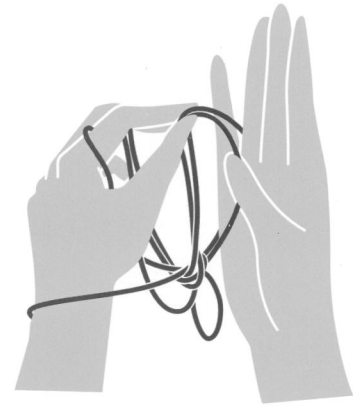

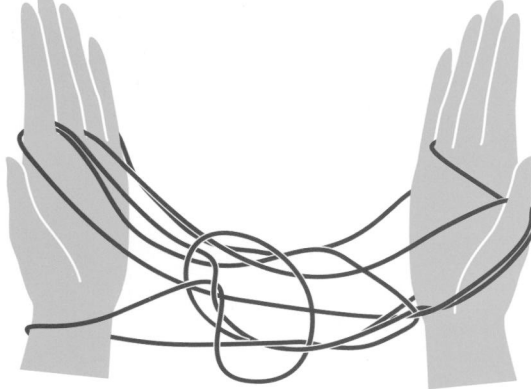

20 Carefully turn your hands with palms towards you, and you'll find that you are left with one loop on your right thumb and another across the first three fingers of your right hand.

21 Repeat the moves made in Steps 16 to 19 but this time in reverse – use your right thumb and index finger to pick up both the strings from your left middle finger. Slip your left hand out of all the loops and your right thumb and index will be left holding two loops as before. Push the little finger of your left hand into the larger of the two loops held by the thumb and index finger of your right, and push your left thumb away from you through both loops. Carefully turn your hands, palms slightly open, but keep the strings relaxed.

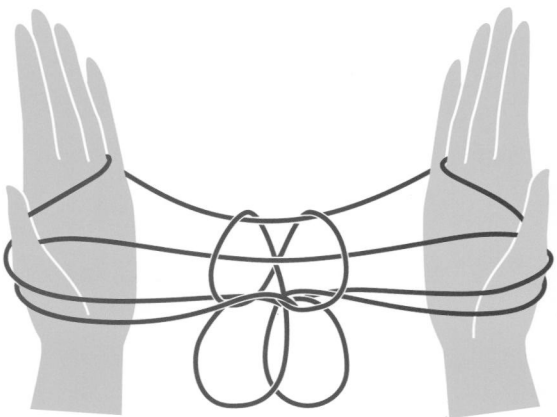

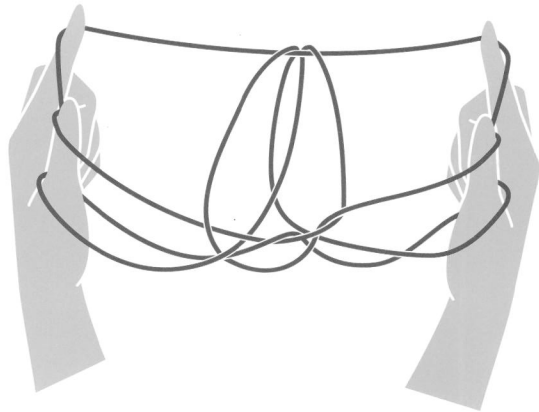

22 Bend your index fingers down and grip the thumb strings furthest from you between the top joints of your index fingers and the top joints of your thumbs. Now use the tips of your index fingers to pick up this further thumb string from underneath.

23 Hold your thumbs close to your index fingers and curl the index fingers towards you and slightly up, turning your palms away from you as you do so. Hold down the furthest little-finger strings with the middle, ring and little fingers of both hands as you pull your hands apart to hold the strings taut. When done correctly the branched coral shape appears as you tighten the strings.

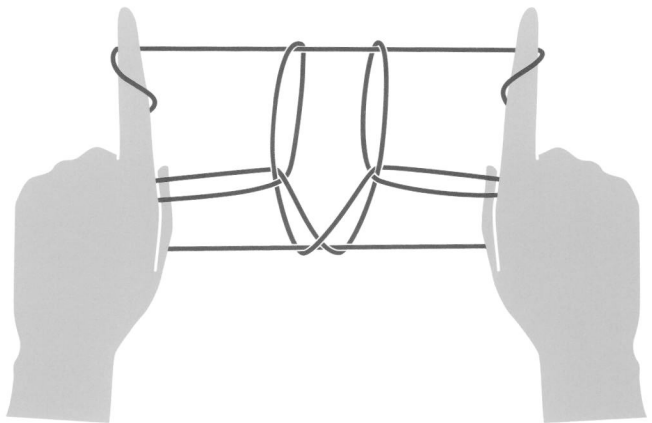

Index

A

Apache Tent 44

C

Candles 13
Caribou, the 81
Caroline Islands Catch 94
Catch-my-Thumb 36
Cat's Cradle 10
    Candles 13
    Cat's Eye 18
    Diamonds 16
    Manger 15
    Soldier's Cot 12
Cat's Eye 18
Coral *see* Coral Reef
Coral Reef 118
Cow's Eyeball *see* Cat's Eye
Crow's Feet *see* Leashing
    the Dogs
Cup and Saucer/Eiffel Tower
    26

D

Diamonds 16
    Two-man Diamonds 76

E

Eiffel Tower *see* Cup and
    Saucer/Eiffel Tower

F

finger nomenclature 7
Fishing Net *see* Jacob's Ladder

H

Hard Cradles 86
    Caroline Islands Catch 94
    Coral Reef 118
    Leashing the Dogs 88
    Owl's Net, the 111
    Rabbit, the 105
    Well, the 100

I

Intestines of a Turtle *see* Torres
    Straits Lizard

J

Jacob's Ladder 70

L

Leashing Lochiel's Dogs *see*
    Leashing the Dogs
Leashing the Dogs 88

M

Man on a Bed 40
Manger 15, 20
Middling Cradles 52
    Caribou, the 81
    Jacob's Ladder 70
    Navajo Bow 54
    Navajo Lightning 62
    Navajo Stars 58
    Torres Straits Lizard 67
    Two-man Diamonds 76
Mirror *see* Candles
Mouse, the 31

N

Navajo Bow 54
Navajo Lightning 62
Navajo Stars 58
Navajo Tent 48

O

Osage Diamonds *see* Jacob's
    Ladder 36
Owl's Net, the 111

P

Pygmy Diamonds *see* Two-man
    Diamonds

R

Rabbit, the 105

S

Simple Cradles 8
    Apache Tent 44
    Catch-my-Thumb 36
    Cat's Cradle 10
    Cup and Saucer/Eiffel Tower
        26
    Man on a Bed 40
    Mouse, the 31
    Navajo Tent 48
    Witch's Broom 22
Soldier's Cot 12

T

Torres Straits Lizard 67
Two-man Diamonds 76

W

Well, the 100
Witch's Broom 22